THE
INSURRECTION
IN DUBLIN

THE
INSURRECTION
IN DUBLIN

BY JAMES STEPHENS

With an Introduction and Afterword
by JOHN A. MURPHY

COLIN SMYTHE
Gerrards Cross, 1992

First published in 1916

This edition copyright © 1978, 1992 by Colin Smythe Ltd.

This edition first published in 1978 by
Colin Smythe Ltd., Gerrards Cross, Buckinghamshire
England
reprinted, with illustrations, 1992

British Library Cataloguing in Publication Data

Stephens, James, b. 1882
The insurrection in Dublin.
1. Ireland — History — Sinn Fein Rebellion, 1916
I. Title
941.5082'1'0924   DA962

ISBN 0–86140–358–4

Printed in Great Britain
by The Guernsey Press Ltd., Vale, Guernsey, C.I.

CONTENTS

ILLUSTRATIONS
between pages 60 and 61

The Insurrection and its aftermath,
chiefly from contemporary postcards.

INTRODUCTION

JOHN A. MURPHY,
Professor of Irish History,
University College, Cork

'THE few chapters which make up this book are not a history of the rising', says James Stephens in his foreword, 'and it may be years before exact information on the subject is available'. That information, and its assessment, did indeed take years. The anniversary year of 1966 resulted in an impressive crop of 1916 studies,[1] and the historian is now in a position to fill in the background to the eye-witness account here being republished, and to assess the Rising in historical perspective.

The dramatic events of Easter Week, 1916, have their genesis in that remarkable turn-of-the century ferment which constitutes a new development in Irish nationalism and which we sometimes call the Irish renaissance. The Gaelic League, the Gaelic Athletic Association, the stimulus of the 1798 centenary, even arguably the works of poets and dramatists

vii

such as Yeats and his circle, all played a role in the formation of a new and heightened national consciousness.

In its political aspect, however, the antecedents of the insurrection can be more narrowly defined. Though the warring factions of Parnell's once great parliamentary party reunited in 1900 under John Redmond, the latter never inherited the allegiance which nationalist Ireland had given to the Chief. The party all too obviously bore the scars of the long internecine strife and young Irish nationalists turned away from what they regarded as the jaded politics of compromise to listen to exciting new voices. The most vital and commanding of these was Arthur Griffith who preached the Sinn Féin (Ourselves Alone) doctrine of political, economic and cultural self-sufficiency for Ireland. Though Sinn Féin as a political organization had little success in the years before 1916, its chief spokesman propagated its tenets with such passion, eloquence and persistence that he more than any other must be regarded as the architect of the new nationalist resurgence. Though Sinn Féin preached non-violence and was by no means committed to a separatist solution of the Irish question, the movement so shaped the separatist mind that the Rising in which it played no organizational role was popularly, if inaccurately, dubbed the Sinn Féin Rebellion by British and native alike.

Thus, while Stephens's first informant tells him that 'the Sinn Féiners' have seized the city, he himself correctly refers throughout to the insurgents as the Volunteers. The Irish Volunteers had been called into existence in the situation that arose from the expected advent of Home Rule. Early in 1913, Northern Unionists, under the leadership of Sir Edward Carson and Sir James Craig, formed themselves into the Ulster Volunteers, with the intention of opposing, in arms if necessary, 'the present conspiracy to set up a Home Rule parliament in Ireland'. Professor Eoin MacNeill, respected academic and co-founder of the Gaelic League, called on nationalist Ireland to follow the Ulster example. Accordingly, the Irish Volunteers were founded on 25 November, 1913 to protect and defend Irish liberties. Their foundation was welcomed by the Irish Republican Brotherhood, a secret

INTRODUCTION

society dating back to 1858 whose aim was the simple and extreme one of establishing an Irish Republic by force of arms. After a period of stagnation, the IRB was revitalized by new men from about 1907 onwards. The Brotherhood was already involved in various nationalist organizations: now it proceeded covertly to infiltrate the Volunteers and manipulate that open body in the direction of rebellion, taking care to maintain a hidden profile.

As the Irish Volunteers swelled in number (180,000 by September, 1914), John Redmond on behalf of the Irish parliamentary party, still the elected political representatives of nationaist Ireland, succeeded in having his own nominees accepted on the provisional committee of the Volunteers. The misgivings of the founding members at this development were very soon justified by Redmond's public reaction to the outbreak of war in Europe. At first, he pledged that the Volunteers would defend Ireland so that the regular forces of the Crown could be withdrawn to fight in Europe: shortly afterwards however, in a speech at Woodenbridge, Co. Wicklow, in September, 1914, he urged the Volunteers to go 'wherever the

INTRODUCTION

firing-line extends'. There now ensued a split in the Volunteers: the great majority followed Redmond and were thenceforth called the National Volunteers while about 11,000 men, retaining the name of the Irish Volunteers, continued to espouse the original aims of the organization and to serve under their commander-founder, Eoin MacNeill. As the 11,000 expanded to about 16,000 by April, 1916, arms and ammunition were secured and the leaders announced their firm intention of resisting any attempt to suppress the Irish Volunteers. At the same time, it was emphasised that their role would continue to be defensive. The toleration of such a body by the authorities, especially in wartime, reflects the disastrously weak and confused Irish policies of the British government as well as the liberal political culture of the United Kingdom.

Meanwhile, the IRB welcomed the arrival of war and the purging of the Volunteers as factors favouring their own plans for rebellion which were now intensified. The Brotherhood set up a Military Council — the seven members eventually comprising it were to be the members of the provisional government in

INTRODUCTION

Easter Week and the signatories of the proclamation—which proceeded in absolute
secrecy to organize an insurrection using the
ready-made organization of the Irish Volunteers. The members of this Council held key
positions in the Volunteers: Patrick Pearse,
in particular, held the vital position of Director
of Organization and was thus able to order
'manoeuvres' for the 1916 Easter weekend, an
ostensibly innocuous operation. Most of the
leading Volunteer officers were IRB men who
were aware of what was afoot. While the pre-
vailing secrecy effectively ensured that the spies
and informers who had sabotaged earlier
rebellions would not this time emerge, it also
inevitably caused the confusion that in the end
turned the rebellion plans into a *débâcle*,
except in Dublin and a few isolated areas.

Easter Sunday, 1916 was the original date
chosen. German arms were to be secured
through the offices of Clan na Gael, the IRB's
supporting organization in the United States.
However, communications were much confused and the commander of the *Aud*, the
German submarine carrying the arms, was
unable to make Irish contact, was intercepted

by British warships, and eventually scuttled his ship off Queenstown Harbour on Saturday, 22 April. Sir Roger Casement, playing out his role of a tragic Don Quixote, was imprisoned soon after he came ashore on a lonely Kerry strand. Within a few months, he was to be tried for treason and executed.

The IRB conspiracy had involved the continual deception of Eoin MacNeill who, as Chief of Staff of the Volunteers, had all along been insistent that the Volunteers would maintain a purely defensive stance and would go into action only if the government tried to suppress them or impose conscription on Irishmen. Almost at the last moment (Thursday, 20 April) he learned that a rising was intended. Confronting Pearse, he declared he would do all in his power to stop it. A little later (Good Friday, 21 April) he yielded to the arguments of Pearse, MacDonagh and Seán Mac Diarmada that it was now too late to reverse the arrangements for the following Sunday, and that any orders he might issue would only make confusion worse confounded. Besides, he learned for the first time that German aid was on its way, and this news was for him a decisive factor. Also at this stage, MacNeill believed in the authenticity of a document purporting to emanate from Dublin Castle and containing instructions for the suppression of the Volunteers (see Stephens's reference, p. 83, to 'the paper which Alderman Kelly read to the Dublin Corporation'). But hard on the heels of MacNeill's consent, he received information (Saturday, 22 April) that the German submarine had come to grief, that Casement had been captured and that the 'Castle document' was a forgery. Now at last aware of the full extent of his deception and convinced that a rebellion in the circumstances was madness, the Chief of Staff publicly countermanded the mobilisation instructions for Sunday. Nevertheless, the Military Council decided to go ahead with the Rising, the time now being changed to Easter Monday (24 April) at noon. The conflicting orders caused widespread confusion among Volunteer commandants throughout the country. As a result, the projected nation-wide scale of insurrection dwindled to a rebellion in Dublin and one or two isolated attempts elsewhere. When the 'blood sacrifice' aspect of the Easter Rising is stressed, it should be remembered that up to the stage of the final confusion, the Military Council believed the rebellion had a real chance of success. It was only when the last desperate decision was taken that sacrificial regeneration took the place of a planned military venture.

The 1,300 or so Volunteers who turned out in Dublin on the Easter Monday bank holiday were joined by a couple of hundred from James Connolly's Irish Citizen Army. The Citizen Army was the outcome of the great strike-lockout of 1913 and it now took the field to fight for Connolly's objective of an Irish socialist republic, though the socialist element was an insignificant one in the nationalist movement generally. Among the Volunteer leaders who responded to the call was The O'Rahilly, who receives honourable mention in Stephens's pages. He was not privy to the counsels of the IRB and had supported Mac-Neill's attempt to stop the Rising but, in the words which Yeats puts into his mouth, 'because I helped to wind the clock, I come to hear it strike'. The reader may be here reminded that James Stephens, like almost everybody else, was ignorant of the IRB's role in the Rising. He was a spectator at the drama and observed the cast of Volunteers but was unaware of the identity of the stage managers.

Given the shambles in which the Rising began, the unrealistic strategy of seizing buildings and waiting to be attacked, and the weakness of the Volunteers in respect of resources and numbers (at the most 1,600 as against 12,000 Crown forces), the wonder is that the insurgents held out for a whole week. The element of surprise was certainly in their favour. In the end, the surrender order was given not only because the position had become hopeless but because the Volunteer leadership wished to avoid the further loss of civilian life. The chivalry and idealism of the insurgents is also apparent in the Proclamation of the Republic which reflects the high-minded rhetoric of nineteenth-century nationalism. The Republic 'declares its resolve to pursue the happiness and prosperity of the whole nation and of all its parts, cherishing all the children of the nation equally, and oblivious of the differences, carefully fostered by an alien government, which have divided a minority from the majority in the past'. The sacred cause is placed under 'the protection of the Most High God . . . and we pray that no one who serves that cause will dishonour it by cowardice, inhumanity, or rapine. In this supreme hour the Irish nation must, by its valour and discipline and by the readiness of its children to sacrifice themselves for the common good, prove itself worthy of the august destiny to which it is called'.

When Pearse, as president of the 'provisional Republic', read the proclamation on Easter Monday from the steps of the General Post Office (the insurgents' general headquarters), he received an indifferent hearing from a small knot of bystanders. However, hostility rather than indifference was the reaction of the average Dubliner and this comes across sharply in Stephens's chronicle of events. Baffled anger at the lunacy of the whole venture was the dominant emotion of the great majority of Irish nationalists who still supported Redmond and the party. There was anger, too, at what seemed the wanton destruction of the capital and the violent disruption of ordinary social and commercial activities. Here again the Stephens narrative faithfully reflects the popular mood. A particularly intense resentment of the insurgents was shown by the 'war widows' and other relatives of those thousands of Dubliners who were fighting on the Western front and against whom this rebellion seemed an unforgivable stab in the back. When the captured Volunteers were marched off to courtmartials and prison camps, they were left in no doubt concerning the antagonistic feelings of Dublin onlookers. Disapproval of the rebellion was also widely voiced in the popular press.

But the tide was soon to turn dramatically. Even in the course of the week itself, as Stephens's observations show, hostility towards the Volunteers came to be tempered a little by a grudging respect for their gallant stand: it was instinctively appreciated, as a matter of local pride, that the insurgents had not shamed the city. But it was the protracted executions in early May that changed popular attitudes 'utterly', to use Yeats's celebrated adverb. As fourteen rebels were tried by court-martial and shot, two or more per day, they were no longer seen as detestable miscreants but as martyred heroes. It was the drawn-out manner of the agony, and the shooting of the wounded Connolly strapped to a chair, that outraged Irish opinion. Once again, British governmental action in Ireland proved more inept than malevolent, since the actual dimensions of the reprisal could hardly be held to be excessively savage, given the authorities' view of the rebellion as a despicable act of sabotage against an empire at war. Dormant nationalist sympathies were further aroused by accounts of the courageous attitudes of the doomed men during their courtmartials and before the firing squads, as well as by the revelation of the patriotic and dedicated lives of people like Pearse and MacDonagh. As had happened after the execution of the 'Manchester Martyrs' in 1867, the emotions of nationalism blended with those of religion. Masses were offered, prayers were said, verses of praise were penned. Insurrection was seen as resurrection and it seemed that the Irish people would fulfil Pearse's prophecy by crowding into the house that he had built in his heart. In short, the scene was set for the resurgence of Sinn Fein.

INTRODUCTION

*   *   *

As poet and writer, James Stephens was very much part of the Irish cultural and political renaissance and of the whole ambience which surrounds the pre-Rising period. He was a contributor to *Sinn Féin*[2] and an admirer of Arthur Griffith,[3] and on his return from Paris to Dublin in September, 1915 to take up his post as Registrar of the National Gallery, he proposed to explore 'the passionate, varied story that Ireland is and has been' so that he might attain 'a consciousness of Ireland in all its dimensions'.[4] There is a sense therefore in which the Rising, for all its dramatic suddenness, was an event for which Stephens was psychologically prepared and to the implications of which he was sensitively attuned. Certainly, the Rising and its aftermath had a profound impact on his work : this is a point convincingly argued by Augustine Martin in a recent biography. In the decade after 1916, says Dr. Martin, Stephens 'devoted his energies to the imaginative recovery of Ireland's poetic and mythological past. There can be little doubt that the impact of the military and political upheaval provided him with a fresh inspiration and pointed the new direction that he had been hoping for in his final letters from Paris'.[5]

In all this, Stephens was extremely fortunate to have been on hand to witness the Rising. The writer as observer of the momentous historical event is a relatively rare phenomenon. One thinks of John Hersey at Hiroshima or Norman Mailer at Chicago, and Stephens's chronicle deserves to rank highly in this unusual journalistic *genre*. He is at his best in the terse and graphic eyewitness descriptions where he makes no attempt to hide the bloody realities of war, but his wry accounts of hearsay and rumour are also full of interest, as are his conversations with such people as Douglas Hyde (D.H.) and Sarah Purser (Miss P.). The writer's attempts to master musical notation in preparation for playing the dulcimer form a comically mundane prelude to the epic event, and this incongruity somehow lends an air of authentic immediacy to the narrative. His thumbnail sketches of the dramatis personae—Pearse, Connolly, Plunkett, MacDonagh, The O'Rahilly, and that 'absurdly courageous' pacifist, Sheehy Skeffington—are imaginative and sympathetic yet perceptive and critical. When he claims that 'the blood of brave men' was necessary to sanctify Irish freedom, he is enunciating a sentiment repugnant to our own generation but perfectly acceptable to a wide circle of nationalists in his own day and by no means peculiar to Patrick Pearse.

In his personal assessments of factors for which he had no background information—the role of Eoin MacNeill, the dimension of German aid, and relative significance of nationalism and socialism—Stephens's snap judgements are impressively sound. The one blind spot is his attack on John Redmond. True, the leader of the Party had grown increasingly out of touch with nationalist developments and his Woodenbridge speech was a major political blunder but Stephens's castigation of Redmond as the villain of the piece is a harsh and biassed judgement as well as an untenable historical interpretation. On the other hand, the writer's warning to English statesmen is prophetic, his plea for Anglo-Irish rapprochement generously rises above the passions of the day and his optimistic hopes for a bright Irish future are bravely inspiring, now as then. Above all, his original and provocative reflections on the Ulster question will strike the modern reader as extremely topical. Here again, he is very hard on the Irish parliamentary party, but he could hardly have foreseen that the party's blindness towards Ulster Unionists would be perpetuated by Sinn Féin and its political successors down to the present day. That is why one reads what Stephens has to say on this subject with a sad sense of *déjà vu*.

*   *   *

'A terrible beauty is born'. For fifty years or more, the Easter Rising remained the sacred drama of modern Irish nationalism, its protagonists uncritically depicted in nationalist historiography as martyred saints and demigods, and their pronouncements reverenced as holy writ. Just as the 1916 Proclamation reduced the complex texture of Irish history down to a single thread of Anglo-Irish struggle, so did the subsequent 1916 cult regard the Rising as the apotheosis of the historical process, and this was manifest in public ritual as well as in the teaching of history in Irish schools. But in the early 1970s, as a response to the Northern troubles, a revisionist view[6] of 1916 became current in certain political circles, and the State itself—or some of its then ministers—began to question the sacrosanct canon of the Rising. It was argued that Easter 1916 and its aftermath had left a *damnosa hereditas* in its glorification of bloodshed, that the Provisional IRA terrorists were simply working out the dynamic implicit in the Rising and following the precedent of an armed minority flouting majority wishes, that they were the real heirs of Pearse and his comrades and that to honour 1916 necessarily involved approval of the Provisionals. Thus, for a time at least, the State suspended its ritual public commemoration of Easter Week. The revisionist thesis ignored the many dissimilarities between 1916 and the Provisionals and by no means found universal acceptance among historians,[7] let alone the public at large. The view of the present writer is that the Easter Rising is one of those rare epic events in the history of a nation which will continue to have

INTRODUCTION

all the perennial appeal, at the very least, of a great myth. For this reason, if for no other, the State will ignore 1916 at its peril.

REFERENCES

1. These include: O. Dudley Edwards and F. Pyle (ed.), *1916: The Easter Rising* (1968); K. B. Nowlan (ed.), *The Making of 1916* (1969); L. Ó Broin, *Dublin Castle and the 1916 Rising* (1966), for the full background to Stephens's reference to Augustine Birrell and Sir Mathew Nathan; L. Ó Broin, *The Chief Secretary, Augustine Birrell* (1969); T. D. Williams (ed.), *The Irish Struggle, 1916-26* (1966); W. I. Thompson, *The Imagination of an Insurrection: Dublin, Easter 1916* (1967); F. X. Martin (ed.), *Leaders and Men of the Easter Rising: Dublin 1916* (1967); F. X. Martin '1916 – Myth, Fact and Mystery', *Studia Hibernica,* 1967; F. X. Martin, 'The 1916 Rising: A *Coup d'État* or a "Bloody Protest" ', *Studia Hibernica*, 1968; F. O'Donoghue, 'The failure of the German arms landing at Easter 1916', *Journal of the Cork Historical and Archaeological Society,* 1966.

   See also Ruth Dudley Edwards, *Patrick Pearse: The Triumph of Failure* (1977), a splendid assessment; M. Caulfield, *The Easter Rebellion* (paperback ed., 1965); B. Hobson, *Ireland Today and Tomorrow* (1968); E. Holt, *Protest in Arms: The Irish Troubles, 1916-23* (1960); D. Lynch, *The*

INTRODUCTION

I.R.B. and the 1916 Rising, ed. F. O'Donoghue (1957); F. X. Martin and F. J. Byrne, *The Scholar Revolutionary, Eoin MacNeill* (1973); D. Ryan, *The Rising: The Complete Story of Easter Week* (3rd ed., 1957).

For an excellent brief account, see the relevant pages in F. S. L. Lyons, *Ireland since the Famine* (1971).

2. His writings in this paper are listed in Birgit Bramsbäck, *James Stephens: A Literary and Bibliographical Study* (Upsala and Dublin, 1959), pp. 159 ff.

3. For his assessment of Griffith, see *Studies*, vol. xi, September, 1922, and a booklet, *Arthur Griffith, Journalist and Statesman* (1924?). Bramsbäck, *op. cit.*, index *sub* Griffith, provides a comprehensive guide to the Stephens-Griffith relationship.

4. James Stephens to Thomas Bodkin, 1 March, 1915, *Letters of James Stephens*, ed. Richard J. Finneran (London, 1974), pp. 153-4.

5. Augustine Martin, *James Stephens: A Critical Study* (Dublin, 1977), p. 107. Dr. Martin's chapter on 'Stephens and the Easter Rising' is of particular value.

6. The much-discussed revisionist essay by Fr Francis Shaw, S.J., 'The Canon of Irish History – A Challenge', pre-dates the Northern troubles. It was intended for publication in 1966 but was withheld until much later: *Studies*, Summer 1972.

7. For a rhapsodically traditional and unashamedly non-revisionist view of 1916 and after, see George Dangerfield, *The Damnable Question* (American ed., 1976: London, 1977).

FOREWORD

THE day before the rising was Easter Sunday, and they were crying joyfully in the Churches "Christ has risen." On the following day they were saying in the streets " Ireland has risen." The luck of the moment was with her. The auguries were good, and, notwithstanding all that has succeeded, I do not believe she must take to the earth again, nor be ever again buried. The pages hereafter were written day by day during the Insurrection that followed Holy Week, and, as a hasty impression of a most singular time, the author allows them to stand without any emendation.

The few chapters which make up this book are not a history of the rising. I knew nothing about the rising. I do not know anything about it now, and it may be years before exact information on the subject is available. What I have written is no more than a statement of what passed in one quarter of our city, and a gathering together of the rumour and tension which for nearly two weeks had to serve the Dublin people in lieu of news. It had to serve many Dublin people in place of bread.

To-day, the 8th of May, the book is finished, and, so far as Ireland is immediately concerned, the insurrection is over. Action now lies with England, and on that action depends whether the Irish Insurrection is over or only suppressed.

In their dealings with this country, English Statesmen have seldom shown political imagination; sometimes they have been just, sometimes, and often, unjust. After a certain point I dislike and despise justice. It is an attribute of God, and is adequately managed by Him alone; but between man and man no other ethics save that of kindness can give results. I have not any hope that this ethic will replace that, and I merely mention it in order that the good people who read these words may enjoy the laugh which their digestion needs.

I have faith in man, I have very little faith in States man. But I believe that the world moves, and I believe that the weight of the rolling planet is going to bring freedom to Ireland. Indeed, I name this date as the first

day of Irish freedom, and the knowledge for-
bids me mourn too deeply my friends who are
dead.

It may not be worthy of mention, but the
truth is, that Ireland is not cowed. She is excited a little. She is gay a little. She was
not with the revolution, but in a few months
she will be, and her heart which was withering will be warmed by the knowledge that
men have thought her worth dying for. She
will prepare to make herself worthy of devotion, and that devotion will never fail her.
So little does it take to raise our hearts.

Does it avail anything to describe these
things to English readers? They have never
moved the English mind to anything except
impatience, but to-day and at this desperate
conjunction they may be less futile than here-
tofore. England also has grown patriotic,
even by necessity. It is necessity alone makes
patriots, for in times of peace a patriot is a
quack when he is not a shark. Idealism pays
in times of peace, it dies in time of war. Our
idealists are dead and yours are dying hourly.

The English mind may to-day be enabled to
understand what is wrong with us, and why

through centuries we have been "disthress-
ful." Let them look at us, I do not say
through the fumes that are still rising from
our ruined streets, but through the smoke that
is rolling from the North Sea to Switzerland,
and read in their own souls the justification
for all our risings, and for this rising.

Is it wrong to say that England has not one
friend in Europe? I say it. Her Allies of
to-day were her enemies of yesterday, and
politics alone will decide what they will be
to-morrow. I say it, and yet I am not entirely
right, for she has one possible friend unless
she should decide that even one friend is excessive and irks her. That one possible friend
is Ireland. I say, and with assurance, that if
our national questions are arranged there will
remain no reason for enmity between the two
countries, and there will remain many reasons
for friendship.

It may be objected that the friendship of
a country such as Ireland has little value;
that she is too small geographically, and too
thinly populated to give aid to any one.
Only sixty odd years ago our population was
close on ten millions of people, nor are we yet

sterile; in area Ireland is not collossal, but neither is she microscopic. Mr. Shaw has spoken of her as a "cabbage patch at the back of beyond." On this kind of description Rome might be called a hen-run and Greece a back yard. The sober fact is that Ireland has a larger geographical area than many an independent and prosperous European kingdom, and for all human and social needs she is a fairly big country, and is beautiful and fertile to boot. She could be made worth knowing if goodwill and trust are available for the task.

I believe that what is known as the "mastery of the seas" will, when the great war is finished, pass irretrievably from the hands or the ambition of any nation, and that more urgently than ever in her history England will have need of a friend. It is true that we might be her enemy and might do her some small harm—it is truer that we could be her friend, and could be of very real assistance to her.

Should the English Statesman decide that our friendship is worth having let him create a little of the political imagination already spoken of. Let him equip us (it is England's debt to Ireland for freedom; not in the manner of a miser who arranges for the chilly livelihood of a needy female relative; but the way a wealthy father would undertake the settlement of his son. I fear I am assisting my reader to laugh too much, but laughter is the sole excess that is wholesome.

If freedom is to come to Ireland—as I believe it is—then the Easter Insurrection was the only thing that could have happened. I speak as an Irishman, and am momentarily leaving out of account every other consideration, If, after all her striving, freedom had come to her as a gift, as a peaceful present such as is sometimes given away with a pound of tea, Ireland would have accepted the gift with shamefacedness, and have felt that her centuries of revolt had ended in something very like ridicule. The blood of brave men had to sanctify such a consummation if the national imagination was to be stirred to the dreadful business which is the organizing of freedom, and both imagination and brains have been stagnant in Ireland this many a year. Following on such tameness, failure might have been predicted, or, at least feared, and war (let us call it war for the sake of our pride) was due to Ireland before she could enter gallantly on her inheritance. We might have crept into liberty like some kind of domesticated man, whereas now we may be allowed to march into freedom with the honours of war. I am still appealing to the political imagination, for if England allows Ireland to formally make peace with her that peace will be lasting, everlasting; but if the liberty you give us is all half-measures, and distrusts and stinginesses, then what is scarcely worth accepting will hardly be worth thanking you for.

There is a reference in the earlier pages of this record to a letter which I addressed to Mr. George Bernard Shaw and published in the *New Age*. This was a thoughtless letter, and subsequent events have proved that it was unmeaning and ridiculous. I have since, through the same hospitable journal, apologised to Mr. Shaw, but have let my reference to the matter stand as an indication that electricity was already in the air. Every statement I made about him in that letter and in this book was erroneous; for, afterwards, when it would have been politic to run for cover, he ran for the open, and he spoke there like the valiant thinker and great Irishman that he is.

Since the foregoing was written events have moved in this country. The situation is no longer the same. The executions have taken place. One cannot justly exclaim against the measures adopted by the military tribunal, and yet, in the interests of both countries one may deplore them. I have said there was no bitterness in Ireland, and it was true at the time of writing. It is no longer true; but it is still possible by generous Statesmanship to allay this, and to seal a true union between Ireland and England.

THE

INSURRECTION IN DUBLIN

CHAPTER I

MONDAY

THIS has taken everyone by surprise. It is possible, that, with the exception of their Staff, it has taken the Volunteers themselves by surprise; but, to-day, our peaceful city is no longer peaceful; guns are sounding, or rolling and crackling from different directions, and, although rarely, the rattle of machine guns can be heard also.

Two days ago war seemed very far away—so far, that I have covenanted with myself to learn the alphabet of music. Tom Bodkin had promised to present me with a musical instrument called a dulcimer—I persist in thinking that this is a species of guitar, although I am assured that it is a number of small metal plates which are struck with sticks, and I confess that this description of its function prejudices me more than a little against it. There is no reason why I should think dubiously of such an instrument, but I do not relish the idea of procuring music with a stick. With this dulcimer I shall be able to tap out our Irish melodies when I am abroad, and transport myself to Ireland for a few minutes, or a few bars.

In preparation for this present I had through Saturday and Sunday been learning the notes of the Scale. The notes and spaces on the lines did not trouble me much, but those above and below the line seemed ingenious and complicated to a degree that frightened me.

On Saturday I got the *Irish Times*, and found in it a long article by Bernard Shaw (reprinted from the *New York Times*). One reads things written by Shaw. Why one does read them I do not know exactly, except that it is a habit we got into years ago, and we read an article by Shaw just as we put on our boots in the morning—that is, without thinking about it, and without any idea of reward.

His article angered me exceedingly. It

was called "Irish Nonsense talked in Ireland." It was written (as is almost all of his journalistic work) with that *bonhomie* which he has cultivated—it is his mannerism—and which is essentially hypocritical and untrue. *Bonhomie*! It is that man-of-the-world attitude, that shop attitude, that between-you-and-me-for-are-we-not-equal-and-cultured attitude, which is the tone of a card-sharper or a trick-of-the-loop man. That was the tone of Shaw's article. I wrote an open letter to him which I sent to the *New Age*, because I doubted that the Dublin papers would print it if I sent it to them, and I knew that the Irish people who read the other papers had never heard of Shaw, except as a trade-mark under which very good Limerick bacon is sold, and that they would not be interested in the opinions of a person named Shaw on any subject not relevant to bacon. I struck out of my letter a good many harsh things which I said of him, and hoped he would reply to it in order that I could furnish these acidities to him in a second letter.

That was Saturday.

On Sunday I had to go to my office, as the

Director was absent in London, and there I applied myself to the notes and spaces below the stave, but relinquished the exercise, convinced that these mysteries were unattainable by man, while the knowledge that above the stave there were others and not less complex, stayed mournfully with me.

I returned home, and as novels (perhaps it is only for the duration of the war) do not now interest me I read for some time in Madame Blavatsky's "Secret Doctrine," which book interests me profoundly. George Russell was out of town or I would have gone round to his house in the evening to tell him what I thought about Shaw, and to listen to his own much finer ideas on that as on every other subject. I went to bed.

On the morning following I awoke into full insurrection and bloody war, but I did not know anything about it. It was Bank Holiday, but for employments such as mine there are not any holidays, so I went to my office at the usual hour, and after transacting what business was necessary I bent myself to the notes above and below the stave, and marvelled anew at the ingenuity of man.

Peace was in the building, and if any of the attendants had knowledge or rumour of war they did not mention it to me.

At one o'clock I went to lunch. Passing the corner of Merrion Row I saw two small groups of people. These people were regarding steadfastly in the direction of St. Stephen's Green Park, and they spoke occasionally to one another with that detached confidence which proved they were mutually unknown. I also, but without approaching them, stared in the direction of the Green. I saw nothing but the narrow street which widened to the Park. Some few people were standing in tentative attitudes, and all looking in the one direction. As I turned from them homewards I received an impression of silence and expectation and excitement.

On the way home I noticed that many silent people were standing in their doorways—an unusual thing in Dublin outside of the back streets. The glance of a Dublin man or woman conveys generally a criticism of one's personal appearance, and is a little hostile to the passer. The look of each person as I passed was steadfast, and contained an enquiry instead of a criticism. I felt faintly uneasy, but withdrew my mind to a meditation which I had covenanted with myself to perform daily, and passed to my house.

There I was told that there had been a great deal of rifle firing all the morning, and we concluded that the Military recruits or Volunteer detachments were practising that arm. My return to business was by the way I had already come. At the corner of Merrion Row I found the same silent groups, who were still looking in the direction of the Green, and addressing each other occasionally with the detached confidence of strangers. Suddenly, and on the spur of the moment, I addressed one of these silent gazers.

" Has there been an accident ? " said I.

I indicated the people standing about.

" What's all this for ? "

He was a sleepy, rough-looking man about 40 years of age, with a blunt red moustache, and the distant eyes which one sees in sailors. He looked at me, stared at me as at a person from a different country. He grew wakeful and vivid.

" Don't you know," said he.

And then he saw that I did not know.

" The Sinn Feiners have seized the City this morning."

" Oh ! " said I.

He continued with the savage earnestness of one who has amazement in his mouth :

" They seized the City at eleven o'clock this morning.   The Green there is full of them. They have captured the Castle.   They have taken the Post Office."

" My God ! " said I, staring at him, and instantly I turned and went running towards the Green.

In a few seconds I banished astonishment and began to walk.   As I drew near the Green rifle fire began like sharply-cracking whips. It was from the further side. I saw that the Gates were closed and men were standing inside with guns on their shoulders. I passed a house, the windows of which were smashed in. As I went by a man in civilian clothes slipped through the Park gates, which instantly closed behind him. He ran towards me, and I halted. He was carrying two small packets in his hand. He passed me hurriedly, and, placing his leg inside the broken window

of the house behind me, he disappeared.
Almost immediately another man in civilian
clothes appeared from the broken window of
another house. He also had something (I
don't know what) in his hand. He ran
urgently towards the gates, which opened,
admitted him, and closed again.

In the centre of this side of the Park a
rough barricade of carts and motor cars had
been sketched. It was still full of gaps.
Behind it was a halted tram, and along the
vistas of the Green one saw other trams
derelict, untenanted.

I came to the barricade. As I reached it
and stood by the Shelbourne Hotel, which it
faced, a loud cry came from the Park. The
gates opened and three men ran out. Two
of them held rifles with fixed bayonets. The
third gripped a heavy revolver in his fist.
They ran towards a motor car which had
just turned the corner, and halted it. The
men with bayonets took position instantly
on either side of the car. The man with the

NOTE—As I pen these words rifle shot is cracking from three
different directions and continually. Three minutes ago there
was two discharges from heavy guns. These are the first heavy
guns used in the Insurrection, 25th April.

8

revolver saluted, and I heard him begging the occupants to pardon him, and directing them to dismount. A man and woman got down. They were again saluted and requested to go to the sidewalk. They did so.

The man crossed and stood by me. He was very tall and thin, middle-aged, with a shaven, wasted face. " I want to get down to Armagh to-day," he said to no one in particular. The loose bluish skin under his eyes was twitching. The Volunteers directed the chauffeur to drive to the barricade and lodge his car in a particular position there. He did it awkwardly, and after three attempts he succeeded in pleasing them. He was a big, brown-faced man, whose knees were rather high for the seat he was in, and they jerked with the speed and persistence of something moved with a powerful spring. His face was composed and fully under command, although his legs were not. He locked the car into the barricade, and then, being a man accustomed to be commanded, he awaited an order to descend. When the order came he walked directly to his master, still preserving all the solemnity of his features. These two men did not address a word to each other, but their drilled and expressionelss eyes were loud with surprise and fear and rage. They went into the Hotel.

I spoke to the man with the revolver. He was no more than a boy, not more certainly than twenty years of age, short in stature, with close curling red hair and blue eyes—a kindly-looking lad. The strap of his sombrero had torn loose on one side, and except while he held it in his teeth it flapped about his chin. His face was sunburnt and grimy with dust and sweat.

This young man did not appear to me to be acting from his reason. He was doing his work from a determination implanted previously, days, weeks perhaps, on his imagination. His mind was—where? It was not with his body. And continually his eyes went searching widely, looking for spaces, scanning hastily the clouds, the vistas of the streets, looking for something that did not hinder him, looking away for a moment from the immediacies and rigours which were impressed where his mind had been.

When I spoke he looked at me, and I know

that for some seconds he did not see me. I said :—

"What is the meaning of all this? What has happened?"

He replied collectedly enough in speech, but with that ramble and errancy clouding his eyes.

"We have taken the City. We are expecting an attack from the military at any moment, and those people," he indicated knots of men, women and children clustered towards the end of the Green, "won't go home for me. We have the Post Office, and the Railways, and the Castle. We have all the City. We have everything."

(Some men and two women drew behind me to listen).

"This morning," said he, "the police rushed us. One ran at me to take my revolver. I fired but I missed him, and I hit a———"

"You have far too much talk," said a voice to the young man.

I turned a few steps away, and glancing back saw that he was staring after me, but I know that he did not see me—he was looking at turmoil, and blood, and at figures that ran towards him and ran away—a world in motion and he in the centre of it astonished.

The men with him did not utter a sound. They were both older. One, indeed, a short, sturdy man, had a heavy white moustache. He was quite collected, and took no notice of the skies, or the spaces. He saw a man in rubbers placing his hand on a motor bicycle in the barricade, and called to him instantly: "Let that alone."

The motorist did not at once remove his hand, whereupon the white-moustached man gripped his gun in both hands and ran violently towards him. He ran directly to him, body to body, and, as he was short and the motorist was very tall, stared fixedly up in his face. He roared up at his face in a mighty voice.

"Are you deaf? Are you deaf? Move back!"

The motorist moved away, pursued by an eye as steady and savage as the point of the bayonet that was level with it.

Another motor car came round the Ely Place corner of the Green and wobbled at the sight of the barricade. The three men who had returned to the gates roared " Halt," but the driver made a tentative effort to turn his wheel. A great shout of many voices came then, and the three men ran to him.

" Drive to the barricade," came the order.

The driver turned his wheel a point further towards escape, and instantly one of the men clapped a gun to the wheel and blew the tyre open. Some words were exchanged, and then a shout :

" Drive it on the rim, drive it."

The tone was very menacing, and the motorist turned his car slowly to the barricade and placed it in.

For an hour I tramped the City, seeing everywhere these knots of watchful strangers speaking together in low tones, and it sank into my mind that what I had heard was true, and that the City was in insurrection. It had been promised for so long, and had been threatened for so long. Now it was here. I had seen it in the Green, others had seen it in other parts—the same men clad in dark green and equipped with rifle, bayonet, and bandolier, the same silent activity. The police had disappeared from the streets. At that hour I did not see one policeman, nor did I see one for many days, and men said that several of them had been shot earlier in the morning; that an officer had been shot on Portobello Bridge, that many soldiers had been killed, and that a good many civilians were dead also.

Around me as I walked the rumour of war and death was in the air. Continually and from every direction rifles were crackling and rolling; sometimes there was only one shot, again it would be a roll of firing crested with single, short explosions, and sinking again to whip-like snaps and whip-like echoes; then for a moment silence, and then again the guns leaped in the air.

The rumour of positions, bridges, public places, railway stations, Government offices, having been seized was persistent, and was not denied by any voice.

I met some few people I knew. P. H., T. M., who said : " Well! " and thrust their eyes into me as though they were rummaging me for information.

But there were not very many people in the streets. The greater part of the population were away on Bank Holiday, and did not know anything of this business. Many of them would not know anything until they found they had to walk home from Kingstown, Dalkey, Howth, or wherever they were.

I returned to my office, decided that I would close it for the day. The men were very relieved when I came in, and were more relieved when I ordered the gong to be sounded. There were some few people in the place, and they were soon put out. The outer gates were locked, and the great door, but I kept the men on duty until the evening. We were the last public institution open; all the others had been closed for hours.

I went upstairs and sat down, but had barely reached the chair before I stood up again, and began to pace my room, to and fro, to and fro; amazed, expectant, inquiet; turning my ear to the shots, and my mind to speculations that began in the middle, and were chased from there by others before they had taken one thought forward. But then I took myself resolutely and sat me down, and I pencilled out exercises above the stave, and

under the stave; and discovered suddenly
that I was again marching the floor, to and
fro, to and fro, with thoughts bursting about
my head as though they were fired on me from
concealed batteries.

At five o'clock I left. I met Miss P., all
of whose rumours coincided with those I had
gathered. She was in exceeding good
humour and interested. Leaving her I met
Cy—, and we turned together up to the Green.
As we proceeded, the sound of firing grew
more distinct, but when we reached the Green
it died away again. We stood a little below
the Shelbourne Hotel, looking at the barricade and into the Park. We could see
nothing. Not a Volunteer was in sight. The
Green seemed a desert. There were only the
trees to be seen, and through them small green
vistas of sward.

Just then a man stepped on the footpath
and walked directly to the barricade. He
stopped and gripped the shafts of a lorry
lodged near the centre. At that instant the
Park exploded into life and sound; from no-
where armed men appeared at the railings,
and they all shouted at the man.

"Put down that lorry. Let out and go away. Let out at once."

These were the cries. The man did not let out. He halted with the shafts in his hand, and looked towards the vociferous pailings. Then, and very slowly, he began to draw the lorry out of the barricade. The shouts came to him again, very loud, very threatening, but he did not attend to them.

"He is the man that owns the lorry," said a voice beside me.

Dead silence fell on the people around while the man slowly drew his cart down by the footpath. Then three shots rang out in succession. At the distance he could not be missed, and it was obvious they were trying to frighten him. He dropped the shafts, and instead of going away he walked over to the Volunteers.

"He has a nerve," said another voice behind me.

The man walked directly towards the Volunteers, who, to the number of about ten, were lining the railings. He walked slowly, bent a little forward, with one hand raised and one finger up as though he were going to make a speech. Ten guns were pointing at him, and a voice repeated many times :

" Go and put back that lorry or you are a dead man. Go before I count four. One, two, three, four——

A rifle spat at him, and in two undulating movements the man sank on himself and sagged to the ground.

I ran to him with some others, while a woman screamed unmeaningly, all on one strident note. The man was picked up and carried to a hospital beside the Arts Club. There was a hole in the top of his head, and one does not know how ugly blood can look until it has been seen clotted in hair. As the poor man was being carried in, a woman plumped to her knees in the road and began not to scream but to screetch.

At that moment the Volunteers were hated. The men by whom I was and who were lifting the body, roared into the railings : —

" We'll be coming back for you, damn you."

From the railings there came no reply, and in an instant the place was again desert and silent, and the little green vistas were slumbering among the trees.

THE INSURRECTION IN DUBLIN

No one seemed able to estimate the number of men inside the Green, and through the day no considerable body of men had been seen, only those who held the gates, and the small parties of threes and fours who arrested motors and carts for their barricades. Among these were some who were only infants—one boy seemed about twelve years of age. He was strutting the centre of the road with a large revolver in his small fist. A motor car came by him containing three men, and in the shortest of time he had the car lodged in his barricade, and dismissed its stupified occupants with a wave of his armed hand.

The knots were increasing about the streets, for now the Bank Holiday people began to wander back from places that were not distant, and to them it had all to be explained anew. Free movement was possible everywhere in the City, but the constant crackle of rifles restricted somewhat that freedom. Up to one o'clock at night belated travellers were straggling into the City, and curious people were wandering from group to group still trying to gather information.

I remained awake until four o'clock in the

morning. Every five minutes a rifle cracked somewhere, but about a quarter to twelve sharp volleying came from the direction of Portobello Bridge, and died away after some time. The windows of my flat listen out towards the Green, and obliquely towards Sackville Street. In another quarter of an hour there were volleys from Stephen's Green direction, and this continued with intensity for about twenty-five minutes. Then it fell into a sputter of fire and ceased.

I went to bed about four o'clock convinced that the Green had been rushed by the military and captured, and that the rising was at an end.

That was the first day of the insurrection.

CHAPTER II

TUESDAY

A SULTRY, lowering day, and dusk skies fat with rain.

I left for my office, believing that the insurrection was at an end. At a corner I asked a man was it all finished. He said it was not, and that, if anything, it was worse.

On this day the rumours began, and I think it will be many a year before the rumours cease. The *Irish Times* published an edition which contained nothing but an official Proclamation that evily-disposed persons had disturbed the peace, and that the situation was well in hand. The news stated in three lines that there was a Sinn Fein rising in Dublin, and that the rest of the country was quiet.

No English or country papers came. There was no delivery or collection of letters. All the shops in the City were shut. There was no traffic of any kind in the streets. There

21

was no way of gathering any kind of information, and rumour gave all the news.

It seemed that the Military and the Government had been taken unawares. It was Bank Holiday, and many military officers had gone to the races, or were away on leave, and prominent members of the Irish Government had gone to England on Sunday.

It appeared that everything claimed on the previous day was true, and that the City of Dublin was entirely in the hands of the Volunteers. They had taken and sacked Jacob's Biscuit Factory, and had converted it into a fort which they held. They had the Post Office, and were building baricades around it ten feet high of sandbags, cases, wire entanglements. They had pushed out all the windows and sandbagged them to half their height, while cart-loads of food, vegetables and ammunition were going in continually. They had dug trenches and were laying siege to one of the city barracks.

It was current that intercourse between Germany and Ireland had been frequent chiefly by means of submarines, which came up near the coast and landed machine guns,

rifles and ammunition. It was believed also
that the whole country had risen, and that
many strong places and cities were in the
hands of the Volunteers. Cork Barracks was
said to be taken while the officers were away
at the Curragh races, that the men without
officers were disorganised, and the place
easily captured.

It was said that Germans, thousands
strong, had landed, and that many Irish
Americans with German officers had arrived
also with full military equipment.

On the previous day the Volunteers had
proclaimed the Irish Republic. This cere-
mony was conducted from the Mansion House
steps, and the manifesto was said to have
been read by Pearse, of St. Enda's. The Republican and Volunteer flag was hoisted on
the Mansion House. The latter consisted of
vertical colours of green, white and orange.
Kerry wireless station was reported captured,
and news of the Republic flashed abroad.
These rumours were flying in the street.

It was also reported that two transports
had come in the night and had landed from
England about 8,000 soldiers. An attack re-

ported on the Post Office by a troop of lancers who were received with fire and repulsed. It is foolish to send cavalry into street war.

In connection with this lancer charge at the Post Office it is said that the people, and especially the women, sided with the soldiers, and that the Volunteers were assailed by these women with bricks, bottles, sticks, to cries of :

" Would you be hurting the poor men ? "

There were other angry ladies who threatened Volunteers, addressing to them this petrifying query :

" Would you be hurting the poor horses ? "

Indeed, the best people in the world live in Dublin.

The lancers retreated to the bottom of Sackville Street, where they remained for some time in the centre of a crowd who were carressing their horses. It may have seemed to them a rather curious kind of insurrection —that is, if they were strangers to Ireland.

In the Post Office neighbourhood the Volunteers had some difficulty in dealing with the people who surged about them while they were preparing the barricade, and hindered them to some little extent. One of the Volunteers was particularly noticeable. He held a lady's umbrella in his hand, and whenever some person became particularly annoying he would leap the barricade and chase his man half a street, hitting him over the head with the umbrella. It was said that the wonder of the world was not that Ireland was at war, but that after many hours the umbrella was still unbroken. A Volunteer night attack on the Quays was spoken of, whereat the military were said to have been taken by surprise and six carts of their ammunition captured. This was probably untrue. Also, that the Volunteers had blown up the Arsenal in the Phœnix Park.

There had been looting in the night about Sackville Street, and it was current that the Volunteers had shot twenty of the looters.

The shops attacked were mainly haberdashers, shoe shops, and sweet shops. Very many sweet shops were raided, and until the end of the rising sweet shops were the favourite mark of the looters. There is something comical in this looting of sweet shops— something almost innocent and child-like.

Possibly most of the looters are children who are having the sole gorge of their lives. They have tasted sweetstuffs they had never toothed before, and will never taste again in this life, and until they die the insurrection of 1916 will have a sweet savour for them.

I went to the Green. At the corner of Merrion Row a horse was lying on the footpath surrounded by blood. He bore two bullet wounds, but the blood came from his throat which had been cut.

Inside the Green railings four bodies could be seen lying on the ground. They were dead Volunteers.

The rain was falling now persistently, and persistently from the Green and from the Shelbourne Hotel snipers were exchanging bullets. Some distance beyond the Shelbourne I saw another Volunteer stretched out on a seat just within the railings. He was not dead, for, now and again, his hand moved feebly in a gesture for aid; the hand was completely red with blood. His face could not be seen. He was just a limp mass, upon which the rain beat pitilessly, and he was sodden and shapeless, and most miserable to see. His companions could not draw him in for the spot was covered by the snipers from th Shelbourne. Bystanders stated that several attempts had already been made to rescue him, but that he would have to remain there until the fall of night.

From Trinity College windows and roof there was also sniping, but the Shelbourne Hotel riflemen must have seriously troubled the Volunteers in the Green.

As I went back I stayed a while in front of the hotel to count the shots that had struck the windows. There were fourteen shots through the ground windows. The holes were clean through, each surrounded by a star—the bullets went through but did not crack the glass. There were three places in which the windows had holes half a foot to a foot wide and high. Here many rifles must have fired at the one moment. It must have been as awkward inside the Shelbourne Hotel as it was inside the Green.

A lady who lived in Baggot Street said she had been up all night, and, with her neighbours, had supplied tea and bread to the soldiers who were lining the street. The officer to whom she spoke had made two or three attacks to draw fire and estimate the Volunteers' positions, numbers, &c., and he told her that he considered there were 3,000 well-armed Volunteers in the Green, and as he had only 1,000 soldiers, he could not afford to deliver a real attack, and was merely containing them.

Amiens Street station reported recaptured by the military; other stations are said to be still in the Volunteers' possession.

The story goes that about twelve o'clock on Monday an English officer had marched into the Post Office and demanded two penny stamps from the amazed Volunteers who were inside. He thought their uniforms were postal uniforms. They brought him in, and he is probably still trying to get a perspective on the occurrence. They had as prisoners in the Post Office a certain number of soldiers, and rumour had it that these men accommodated themselves quickly to duress, and were busily engaged peeling potatoes for the meal which they would partake of later on with the Volunteers.

Earlier in the day I met a wild individual who spat rumour as though his mouth were a machine gun or a linotype machine. He believed everything he heard; and everything he heard became as by magic favourable to his hopes, which were violently anti-English. One unfavourable rumour was instantly crushed by him with three stories which were favourable and triumphantly so. He said the Germans had landed in three places. One of these landings alone consisted of fifteen thousand men. The other landings probably beat that figure. The whole City of Cork was in the hands of the Volunteers, and, to that extent, might be said to be peaceful. German warships had defeated the English, and their transports were speeding from every side. The whole country was up, and the garrison was out-numbered by one hundred to one. These Dublin barracks which had not been taken were now besieged and on the point of surrender.

I think this man created and winged every rumour that flew in Dublin, and he was the sole individual whom I heard definitely taking a side. He left me, and, looking back, I saw him pouring his news into the ear of a gaping stranger whom he had arrested for the purpose. I almost went back to hear would he tell the same tale or would he elaborate it into a new thing, for I am interested in the art of story-telling.

At eleven o'clock the rain ceased, and to it succeeded a beautiful night, gusty with wind, and packed with sailing clouds and stars. We were expecting visitors this night, but the sound of guns may have warned most people away. Three only came, and with them we listened from my window to the guns at the Green challenging and replying to each other, and to where, further away, the Trinity snipers were crackling, and beyond again to the sounds of war from Sackville Street. The firing was fairly heavy, and often the short rattle of machine guns could be heard.

One of the stories told was that the Volunteers had taken the South Dublin Union Workhouse, occupied it, and trenched the grounds. They were heavily attacked by the military, who, at a loss of 150 men, took the place. The tale went that towards the close the officer in command offered them terms of surrender, but the Volunteers replied that they were not there to surrender. They were there to be killed. The garrison consisted of fifty men, and the story said that fifty men were killed.

CHAPTER III

IT was three o'clock before I got to sleep last night, and during the hours machine guns and rifle firing had been continuous.

This morning the sun is shining brilliantly, and the movement in the streets possesses more of animation than it has done. The movement ends always in a knot of people, and folk go from group to group vainly seeking information, and quite content if the rumour they presently gather differs even a little from the one they have just communicated.

The first statement I heard was that the Green had been taken by the military; the second that it had been re-taken; the third that it had not been taken at all. The facts at last emerged that the Green had not been occupied by the soldiers, but that the Volunteers had retreated from it into a house which commanded it. This was found to be the

32

College of Surgeons, and from the windows and roof of this College they were sniping. A machine gun was mounted on the roof; other machine guns, however, opposed them from the roofs of the Shelbourne Hotel, the United Service Club, and the Alexandra Club. Thus a triangular duel opened between these positions across the trees of the Park.

Through the railings of the Green some rifles and bandoliers could be seen lying on the ground, as also the deserted trenches and snipers' holes. Small boys bolted in to see these sights and bolted out again with bullets quickening their feet. Small boys do not believe that people will really kill them, but small boys were killed.

The dead horse was still lying stiff and lamentable on the footpath.

This morning a gunboat came up the Liffey and helped to bombard Liberty Hall. The Hall is breeched and useless. Rumour says that it was empty at the time, and that Connolly with his men had marched long before to the Post Office and the Green. The same source of information relates that three thousand Volunteers came from Belfast on

an excursion train and that they marched
into the Post Office.

On this day only one of my men came in.
He said that he had gone on the roof and had
been shot at, consequently that the Volunteers
held some of the covering houses. I went to
the roof and remained there for half an hour.
There were no shots, but the firing from the
direction of Sackville Street was continuous
and at times exceedingly heavy.

To-day the *Irish Times* was published. It
contained a new military proclamation, and a
statement that the country was peaceful, and
told that in Sackville Street some houses were
burned to the ground.

On the outside railings a bill proclaiming
Martial Law was posted.

Into the newspaper statement that peace
reigned in the country one was inclined to
read more of disquietude than of truth, and
one said is the country so extraordinarily
peaceful that it can be dismissed in three
lines. There is too much peace or too much
reticence, but it will be some time before we
hear from outside of Dublin.

Meanwhile the sun was shining. It was a

delightful day, and the streets outside and around the areas of fire were animated and even gay. In the streets of Dublin there were no morose faces to be seen. Almost everyone was smiling and attentive, and a democratic feeling was abroad, to which our City is very much a stranger; for while in private we are a sociable and talkative people we have no street manners or public ease whatever. Every person spoke to every other person, and men and women mixed and talked without constraint.

Was the City for or against the Volunteers? Was it for the Volunteers, and yet against the rising? It is considered now (writing a day or two afterwards) that Dublin was entirely against the Volunteers, but on the day of which I write no such certainty could be put forward. There was a singular reticence on the subject. Men met and talked volubly, but they said nothing that indicated a personal desire or belief. They asked for and exchanged the latest news, or, rather, rumour, and while expressions were frequent of astonishment at the suddenness and completeness of the occurrence, no expression of opinion for or against was anywhere formulated.

Sometimes a man said, "They will be beaten of course," and, as he prophesied, the neighbour might surmise if he did so with a sad heart or a merry one, but they knew nothing and asked nothing of his views, and themselves advanced no flag.

This was among the men.

The women were less guarded, or, perhaps, knew they had less to fear. Most of the female opinion I heard was not alone unfavourable but actively and viciously hostile to the rising. This was noticeable among the best dressed class of our population; the worst dressed, indeed the female dregs of Dublin life, expressed a like antagonism, and almost in similar language. The view expressed was—

"I hope every man of them will be shot."

And—

"They ought to be all shot."

Shooting, indeed, was proceeding everywhere. During daylight, at least, the sound is not sinister nor depressing, and the thought that perhaps a life had exploded with that crack is not depressing either.

THE INSURRECTION IN DUBLIN

In the last two years of world-war our ideas on death have undergone a change. It is not now the furtive thing that crawled into your bed and which you fought with pill-boxes and medicine bottles. It has become again a rider of the wind whom you may go coursing with through the fields and open places. All the morbidity is gone, and the sickness, and what remains to Death is now health and excitement. So Dublin laughed at the noise of its own bombardment, and made no moan about its dead—in the sunlight. Afterwards—in the rooms, when the night fell, and instead of silence that mechanical barking of the maxims and the whistle and screams of the rifles, the solemn roar of the heavier guns, and the red glare covering the sky. It is possible that in the night Dublin did not laugh, and that she was gay in the sunlight for no other reason than that the night was past.

On this day fighting was incessant at Mount Street Bridge. A party of Volunteers had seized three houses covering the bridge and converted these into forts. It is reported that military casualties at this point were

very heavy. The Volunteers are said also to
hold the South Dublin Union. The soldiers
have seized Guinness's Brewery, while their
opponents have seized another brewery in the
neighbourhood, and betwen these two there is
a continual fusilade.

Fighting is brisk about Ringsend and
along the Canal. Dame Street was said to be
held in many places by the Volunteers. I
went down Dame Street, but saw no Volunteers, and did not observe any sniping from
the houses. Further, as Dame Street is entirely commanded by the roofs and windows
of Trinity College, it is unlikely that they
should be here.

It was curious to observe this, at other
times, so animated street, broad and deserted,
with at the corners of side streets small
knots of people watching. Seen from behind,
Grattan's Statue in College Green seemed
almost alive, and he had the air of addressing
warnings and reproaches to Trinity College.

The Proclamation issued to-day warns all
people to remain within doors until five
o'clock in the morning, and after seven o'clock
at night.

THE INSURRECTION IN DUBLIN

It is still early. There is no news of any kind, and the rumours begin to catch quickly on each other and to cancel one another out. Dublin is entirely cut off from England, and from the outside world. It is, just as entirely cut off from the rest of Ireland; no news of any kind filters in to us. We are land-locked and sea-locked, but, as yet, it does not much matter.

Meantime the belief grows that the Volunteers may be able to hold out much longer than had been imagined. The idea at first among the people had been that the insurrection would be ended the morning after it had began. But to-day, the insurrection having lasted three days, people are ready to conceive that it may last for ever. There is almost a feeling of gratitude towards the Volunteers because they are holding out for a little while, for had they been beaten the first or second day the City would have been humiliated to the soul.

People say: "Of course, they will be beaten." The statement is almost a query, and they continue, "but they are putting up a decent fight." For being beaten does not greatly matter in Ireland, but not fighting does matter. " They went forth always to the battle; and they always fell," Indeed, the history of the Irish race is in that phrase.

The firing from the roofs of Trinity College became violent. I crossed Dame Street some distance up, struck down the Quays, and went along these until I reached the Ballast Office. Further than this it was not possible to go, for a step beyond the Ballast Office would have brought one into the unending stream of lead that was pouring from Trinity and other places. I was looking on O'Connell Bridge and Sackville Street, and the house facing me was Kelly's—a red-brick fishing tackle shop, one half of which was on the Quay and the other half in Sackville Street. This house was being bombarded.

I counted the report of six different machine guns which played on it. Rifles innumerable and from every sort of place were potting its windows, and at intervals of about half a minute the shells from a heavy gun lobbed in through its windows or thumped mightily against its walls.

For three hours that bombardment continued, and the walls stood in a cloud of red dust and smoke. Rifle and machine gun bullets pattered over every inch of it, and, unfailingly the heavy gun pounded its shells through the windows.

One's heart melted at the idea that human beings were crouching inside that volcano of death, and I said to myself, "Not even a fly can be alive in that house."

No head showed at any window, no rifle cracked from window or roof in reply. The house was dumb, lifeless, and I thought every one of those men are dead.

It was then, and quite suddenly, that the possibilities of street fighting flashed on me, and I knew there was no person in the house, and said to myself, "They have smashed through the walls with a hatchet and are sitting in the next house, or they have long ago climbed out by the skylight and are on a roof half a block away." Then the thought came to me—they have and hold the entire of Sackville Street down to the Post Office. Later on this proved to be the case, and I knew at this moment that Sackville Street was doomed.

I continued to watch the bombardment, but no longer with the anguish which had before torn me. Near by there were four men, and a few yards away, clustered in a laneway, there were a dozen others. An agitated girl was striding from the farther group to the one in which I was, and she addressed the men in the most obscene language which I have ever heard. She addressed them man by man, and she continued to speak and cry and scream at them with all that obstinate, angry patience of which only a woman is capable.

She cursed us all. She called down diseases on every human being in the world excepting only the men who were being bombarded. She demanded of the folk in the laneway that they should march at least into the roadway and prove that they were proud men and were not afraid of bullets. She had been herself into the danger zone. Had stood herself in the track of the guns, and had there cursed her fill for half an hour, and she desired that the men should do at least what she had done.

This girl was quite young—about nineteen

years of age—and was dressed in the customary shawl and apron of her class. Her face was rather pretty, or it had that pretty slenderness and softness of outline which belong to youth. But every sentence she spoke contained half a dozen indecent words. Alas, it was only that her vocabulary was not equal to her emotions, and she did not know how to be emphatic without being obscene— it is the cause of most of the meaningless swearing one hears every day. She spoke to me for a minute, and her eyes were as soft as those of a kitten and her language was as gentle as her eyes. She wanted a match to light a cigarette, but I had none, and said that I also wanted one. In a few minutes she brought me a match, and then she recommenced her tireless weaving of six vile words into hundreds of stupid sentences.

About five o'clock the guns eased off of Kelly's.

To inexperienced eyes they did not seem to have done very much damage, but afterwards one found that although the walls were standing and apparently solid there was no inside to the house. From roof to basement the build ing was bare as a dog kennel. There were no floors inside, there was nothing there but blank space; and on the ground within was the tumble and rubbish that had been roof and floors and furniture. Everything inside was smashed and pulverised into scrap and dust, and the only objects that had consistency and their ancient shape were the bricks that fell when the shells struck them.

Rifle shots had begun to strike the house on the further side of the street, a jewellers' shop called Hopkins & Hopkins. The impact of these balls on the bricks was louder than the sound of the shot which immediately succeeded, and each bullet that struck brought down a shower of fine red dust from the walls. Perhaps thirty or forty shots in all were fired at Hopkins', and then, except for an odd crack, firing ceased.

During all this time there had been no reply from the Volunteers, and I thought they must be husbanding their ammunition, and so must be short of it, and that it would be only a matter of a few days before the end. All this, I said to myself, will be finished in a few days, and they will be finished; life here

44

will recommence exactly where it left off, and except for some newly-filled graves, all will be as it had been until they become a tradition and enter the imagination of their race.

I spoke to several of the people about me, and found the same willingness to exchange news that I had found elsewhere in the City, and the same reticences as regarded their private opinions. Two of them, indeed, and they were the only two I met with during the insurrection, expressed, although in measured terms, admiration for the Volunteers, and while they did not side with them they did not say anything against them. One was a labouring man, the other a gentleman. The remark of the latter was:

" I am an Irishman, and (pointing to the shells that were bursting through the windows in front of us) I hate to see that being done to other Irishmen."

He had come from some part of the country to spend the Easter Holidays in Dublin, and was unable to leave town again.

The labouring man—he was about fifty-six years of age—spoke very quietly and col-

lectedly about the insurrection. He was a
type with whom I had come very little in contact, and I was surprised to find how simple
and good his speech was, and how calm his
ideas. He thought labour was in this movement to a greater extent than was imagined.
I mentioned that Liberty Hall had been
blown up, and that the garrison had either
surrendered or been killed. He replied that
a gunboat had that morning come up the
river and had blown Liberty Hall into smash,
but, he added, there were no men in it. All
the Labour Volunteers had marched with
Connolly into the Post Office.

He said the Labour Volunteers might possibly number about one thousand men, but
that it would be quite safe to say eight hundred, and he held that the Labour Volunteers, or the Citizens' Army, as they called
themselves, had always been careful not to
reveal their numbers. They had always announced that they possessed about two hundred and fifty men, and had never paraded
any more than that number at any one time.
Workingmen, he continued, knew that the
men who marched were always different men.

The police knew it, too, but they thought that the Citizens Army was the *most deserted-from force* in the world.

The men, however, were not deserters—you don't, he said, desert a man like Connolly, and they were merely taking their turn at being drilled and disciplined. They were raised against the police who, in the big, strike of two years ago, had acted towards them with unparallelled savagery, and the men had determined that the police would never again find them thus disorganised.

This man believed that every member of the Citizen Army had marched with their leader.

" The men, I know," said he, " would not be afraid of anything, and," he continued, " they are in the Post Office now."

" What chance have they ? "

" None," he replied, " and they never said they had, and they never thought they would have any."

" How long do you think they'll be able to hold out ? "

He nodded towards the house that had been bombarded bv heavy guns.

"That will root them out of it quick enough," was his reply.

"I'm going home," said he then, "the people will be wondering if I'm dead or alive," and he walked away from that sad street, as I did myself a few minutes afterwards.

CHAPTER IV.

THURSDAY.

AGAIN, the rumours greeted one. This place had fallen and had ñot fallen. Such a position had been captured by the soldiers; recaptured by the Volunteers, and had not been attacked at all. But certainly fighting was proceeding. Up Mount Street, the rifle volleys were continuous, and the coming and going of ambulance cars from that direction were continuous also. Some spoke of pitched battles on the bridge, and said that as yet the advantage lay with the Volunteers.

At 11.30 there came the sound of heavy guns firing in the direction of Sackville Street. I went on the roof, and remained there for some time. From this height the sounds could be heard plainly. There was sustained firing along the whole central line of the City, from the Green down to Trinity College, and from thence to Sackville Street, and the report of the various types of arm could be easily distinguished. There were rifles, machine guns and very heavy cannon. There was another sound which I could not put a name to, something that coughed out over all the other sounds, a short, sharp bark, or rather a short noise something like the popping of a tremendous cork.

I met D. H. His chief emotion is one of astonishment at the organizing powers displayed by the Volunteers. We have exchanged rumours, and found that our equipment in this direction is almost identical. He says Sheehy Skeffington has been killed. That he was arrested in a house wherein arms were found, and was shot out of hand.

I hope this is another rumour, for, so far as my knowledge of him goes, he was not with the Volunteers, and it is said that he was antagonistic to the forcible methods for which the Volunteers stood. But the tale of his death is so persistent that one is inclined to believe it.

He was the most absurdly courageous man I have ever met with or heard of. He has been in every trouble that has touched Ireland these ten years back, and he has always been in on the generous side, therefore, and

THE INSURRECTION IN DUBLIN

Among the rumours it was stated with every accent of certitude that Madame Markievicz had been captured in George's Street, and taken to the Castle. It was also current that Sir Roger Casement had been captured at sea and had already been shot in the Tower of London. The names of several Volunteer Leaders are mentioned as being dead. But the surmise that steals timidly from one mouth flies boldly as a certitude from every mouth that repeats it, and truth itself would now be listened to with only a gossip's ear, but no person would believe a word of it.

This night also was calm and beautiful, but this night was the most sinister and woeful of those that have passed. The sound of artillery, of rifles, machine guns, grenades, did not cease even for a moment. From my window I saw a red flare that crept to the sky, and stole over it and remained there glaring; the smoke reached from the ground to the clouds, and I could see great red sparks go soaring to enormous heights; while always, in the calm air, hour after hour there was the buzzing and rattling and thudding of guns, and, but for the guns, silence.

THE INSURRECTION IN DUBLIN

It is in a dead silence this Insurrection is being fought, and one imagines what must be the feeling of these men, young for the most part, and unused to violence, who are submitting silently to the crash and flame and explosion by which they are surrounded.

CHAPTER V.

FRIDAY.

THIS morning there are no newspapers, no bread, no milk, no news. The sun is shining, and the streets are lively but discreet. All people continue to talk to one another without distinction of class, but nobody knows what any person thinks.

It is a little singular the number of people who are smiling. I fancy they were listening to the guns last night, and they are smiling this morning because the darkness is past, and because the sun is shining, and because they can move their limbs in space, and may talk without having to sink their voices to a whisper. Guns do not sound so bad in the day as they do at night, and no person can feel lonely while the sun shines.

The men are smiling, but the women laugh, and their laughter does not displease, for whatever women do in whatever circumstances appears to have a rightness of its own.

55

It seems right that they should scream when danger to themselves is imminent, and it seems right that they should laugh when the danger only threatens others.

It is rumoured this morning that Sackville Street has been burned out and levelled to the ground. It is said that the end is in sight; and, it is said, that matters are, if anything rather worse than better. That the Volunteers have sallied from some of their strongholds and entrenched themselves, and that in one place alone (the South Lotts) they have seven machine guns. That when the houses which they held became untenable they rushed out and seized other houses, and that, pursuing these tactics, there seemed no reason to believe that the Insurrection would ever come to an end. That the streets are filled with Volunteers in plain clothes, but having revolvers in their pockets. That the streets are filled with soldiers equally revolvered and plain clothed, and that the least one says on any subject the less one would have to answer for.

The feeling that I tapped was definitely Anti-Volunteer, but the number of people who would speak was few, and one regarded the noncommital folk who were so smiling and polite, and so prepared to talk, with much curiosity, seeking to read in their eyes, in their bearing, even in the cut of their clothes what might be the secret movements and cogitations of their minds.

I received the impression that numbers of them did not care a rap what way it went; and that others had ceased to be mental creatures and were merely machines for registering the sensations of the time.

None of these people were prepared for Insurrection. The thing had been sprung on them so suddenly that they were unable to take sides, and their feeling of detachment was still so complete that they would have betted on the business as if it had been a horse race or a dog fight.

Many English troops have been landed each night, and it is believed that there are more than sixty thousand soldiers in Dublin alone, and that they are supplied with every offensive contrivance which military art has invented.

Merrion Square is strongly held by the

soldiers. They are posted along both sides of the road at intervals of about twenty paces, and their guns are continually barking up at the roofs which surround them in the great square. It is said that these roofs are held by the Volunteers from Mount Street Bridge to the Square, and that they hold in like manner wide stretches of the City.

They appear to have mapped out the roofs with all the thoroughness that had hitherto been expended on the roads, and upon these roofs they are so mobile and crafty and so much at home that the work of the soldiers will be exceedingly difficult as well as dangerous.

Still, and notwithstanding, men can only take to the roofs for a short time. Up there, there can be no means of transport, and their ammunition, as well as their food, will very soon be used up. It is the beginning of the end, and the fact that they have to take to the roofs, even though that be in their programme, means that they are finished.

From the roof there comes the sound of machine guns. Looking towards Sackville Street one picks out easily Nelson's Pillar, which towers slenderly over all the buildings of the neighbourhood. It is wreathed in smoke. Another towering building was the D.B.C. Café. Its Chinese-like pagoda was a landmark easily to be found, but to-day I could not find it. It was not there, and I knew that, even if all Sackville Street was not burned down, as rumour insisted, this great Café had certainly been curtailed by its roof and might, perhaps, have been completely burned.

On the gravel paths I found pieces of charred and burnt paper. These scraps must have been blown remarkably high to have crossed all the roofs that lie between Sackville Street and Merrion Square.

At eleven o'clock there is continuous firing, and snipers firing from the direction of Mount Street, and in every direction of the City these sounds are being duplicated.

In Camden Street the sniping and casualties are said to have been very heavy. One man saw two Volunteers taken from a house by the soldiers. They were placed kneeling in the centre of the road, and within one minute of their capture they were dead.

Simultaneously there fell several of the firing party.

An officer in this part had his brains blown into the roadway. A young girl ran into the road picked up his cap and scraped the brains into it. She covered this poor debris with a little straw, and carried the hat piously to the nearest hospital in order that the brains might be buried with their owner.

The continuation of her story was less gloomy although it affected the teller equally.

" There is not," said she, " a cat or a dog left alive in Camden Street. They are lying stiff out in the road and up on the roofs. There's lots of women will be sorry for this war," said she, " and their pets killed on them."

In many parts of the City hunger began to be troublesome. A girl told me that her family, and another that had taken refuge with them, had eaten nothing for three days. On this day her father managed to get two loaves of bread somewhere, and he brought these home.

" When," said the girl, " my father came in with the bread the whole fourteen of us ran at him, and in a minute we were all

After the Insurrection.—
Corner of Bachelor's Walk and Lr. Sackville Street
which commanded O'Connell Bridge.

Surrender Of P.H. Pearse, April, 29, 1916.

Irish Rebellion _ May 1916
Sackville Street in Flames _ A Photograph taken by a
"Daily Sketch" Photographer under fire.

THE SINN FEIN REVOLT IN DUBLIN.
THE METROPOLE HOTEL, POST OFFICE AND NELSON COLUMN.

ROTARY PHOTO.

After the Insurrection.—Interior General Post Office, Dublin.

Irish Rebellion - May 1916
The General Post Office, Dublin (Rebel Headquarters)
destroyed

RUINS IN SACKVILLE ST. DUBLIN   CHANCELLOR, DUBL

HENRY ST. LOOKING EAST, DUBLIN.

VIEW OF HENRY STREET, DUBLIN.

CHANCELLOR, DUBLIN.

Irish Rebellion May 1916
Sackville Street
in ruins.

MID ABBEY St. FROM LOWER SACKVILLE St. DUBLIN.

ABBEY STREET, DUBLIN.   CHANCELLOR, DUBLIN.

METROPOLE HOTEL DUBLIN   KEOGH BROS.

Irish Rebellion May 1916
The interior of the Ballroom, Imperial
Hotel, Dublin, after the Siege.

Irish Rebellion _ May 1916.
The wreck they made of Church Street, Dublin.

NORTH EARL St FROM NELSON PILLAR, DUBLIN.

CORNER OF SACKVILLE ST. & EDEN QUAY, DUBLIN   CHANCELLOR, DUBLIN

After the Insurrection.—Ruins of Eden Quay

Irish Rebellion. May 1916.
Ruined Sackville Street. Dublin barricaded with Motor Cars

CHANCELLOR DUBLIN   LIBERTY HALL. HEAD-QUARTERS OF CITIZEN ARMY, DUBLIN.

Irish Rebellion—May 1916.
*Talbot Street, Dublin, held against a rebel charge.
Picture taken under fire.*

Irish Rebellion. May 1916.
Soldiers holding a Dublin Street.

Irish Rebellion — May 1916.
Soldiers bivouacking opposite Liberty Hall,
the Rebel Headquarters in Dublin.

Irish Rebellion — May 1916.
A group of Officers with the captured rebel flag.

ashamed for the loaves were gone to the last crumb, and we were all as hungry as we had been before he came in. The poor man,'' said she, '' did not even get a bit for himself.'' She held that the poor people were against the Volunteers.

The Volunteers still hold Jacob's Biscuit Factory. It is rumoured that a priest visited them and counselled surrender, and they replied that they did not go there to surrender but to be killed. They asked him to give them absolution, and the story continues that he refused to do so—but this is not (in its latter part) a story that can easily be credited. The Adelaide Hospital is close to this factory, and it is possible that the proximity of the hospital, delays or hinders military operations against the factory.

Rifle volleys are continuous about Merrion Square, and prolonged machine gun firing can be heard also.

During the night the firing was heavy from almost every direction; and in the direction of Sackville Street a red glare told again of fire.

It is hard to get to bed these nights. It is

hard even to sit down, for the moment one does sit down one stands immediately up again resuming that ridiculous ship's march from the window to the wall and back. I am foot weary as I have never been before in my life, but I cannot say that I am excited. No person in Dublin is excited, but there exists a state of tension and expectancy which is mentally more exasperating than any excitement could be. The absence of news is largely responsible for this. We do not know what has happened, what is happening, or what is going to happen, and the reversion to barbarism (for barbarism is largely a lack of news) disturbs us.

Each night we have got to bed at last murmuring, "I wonder will it be all over to-morrow," and this night the like question accompanied us.

CHAPTER VI.

SATURDAY.

THIS morning also there has been no bread, no milk, no meat, no newspapers, but the sun is shining. It is astonishing that, thus early in the Spring, the weather should be so beautiful.

It is stated freely that the Post Office has been taken, and just as freely it is averred that it has not been taken. The approaches to Merrion Square are held by the military, and I was not permitted to go to my office. As I came to this point shots were fired at a motor car which had not stopped on being challenged. Bystanders said it was Sir Horace Plunkett's car, and that he had been shot. Later we found that Sir Horace was not hurt, but that his nephew who drove the car had been severely wounded.

At this hour the rumour of the fall of Verdun was persistent. Later on it was denied, as was denied the companion rumour of the relief of Kut. Saw R. who had spent three days and the whole of his money in getting home from County Clare. He had heard that Mrs. Sheehy Skeffington's house was raided, and that two dead bodies had been taken out of it. Saw Miss P. who seemed sad. I do not know what her politics are, but I think that the word " kindness " might be used to cover all her activities. She has a heart of gold, and the courage of many lions. I then met Mr. Commissioner Bailey who said the Volunteers had sent a deputation, and that terms of surrender were being discussed. I hope this is true, and I hope mercy will be shown to the men. Nobody believes there will be any mercy shown, and it is freely reported that they are shot in the street, or are taken to the nearest barracks and shot there. The belief grows that no person who is now in the Insurrection will be alive when the Insurrection is ended.

That is as it will be. But these days the thought of death does not strike on the mind with any severity, and, should the European war continue much longer, the fear of death will entirely depart from man, as it has de-

parted many times in history. With that
great deterrent gone our rulers will be gravely
at a loss in dealing with strikers and other
such discontented people. Possibly they will
have to resurrect the long-buried idea of tor-
ture.

The people in the streets are laughing and
chatting. Indeed, there is gaiety in the air
as well as sunshine, and no person seems to
care that men are being shot every other
minute, or bayoneted, or blown into scraps
or burned into cinders. These things are
happening, nevertheless, but much of their
importance has vanished.

I met a man at the Green who was drawing
a plan on the back of an envelope. The
problem was how his questioner was to get
from where he was standing to a street lying
at the other side of the river, and the plan as
drawn insisted that to cover this quarter of
an hour's distance he must set out on a
pilgrimage of more than twenty miles. Another young boy was standing near embracing
a large ham. He had been trying for three
days to convey his ham to a house near the
Gresham Hotel where his sister lived. He

had almost given up hope, and he hearkened intelligently to the idea that he should himself eat the ham and so get rid of it.

The rifle fire was persistent all day, but, saving in certain localities, it was not heavy. Occasionally the machine guns rapped in. There was no sound of heavy artillery.

The rumour grows that the Post Office has been evacuated, and that the Volunteers are at large and spreading everywhere across the roofs. The rumour grows also that terms of surrender are being discussed, and that Sackville Street has been levelled to the ground.

At half-past seven in the evening calm is almost complete. The sound of a rifle shot being only heard at long intervals.

I got to bed this night earlier than usual. At two o'clock I left the window from which a red flare is yet visible in the direction of Sackville Street. The morning will tell if the Insurrection is finished or not, but at this hour all is not over. Shots are ringing all around and down my street, and the vicious crackling of these rifles grow at times into regular volleys.

CHAPTER VII.

SUNDAY.

THE Insurrection has not ceased.

There is much rifle fire, but no sound from the machine guns or the eighteen pounders and trench mortars.

From the window of my kitchen the flag of the Republic can be seen flying afar. This is the flag that flies over Jacob's Biscuit Factory, and I will know that the Insurrection has ended as soon as I see this flag pulled down.

When I went out there were few people in the streets. I met D. H., and, together, we passed up the Green. The Republican flag was still flying over the College of Surgeons. We tried to get down Grafton Street (where broken windows and two gaping interiors told of the recent visit of looters), but a little down this street we were waved back by armed sentries. We then cut away by the Gaiety Theatre into Mercer's Street, where immense lines of poor people were drawn up waiting for the opening of the local bakery. We got into George's Street, thinking to turn down Dame Street and get from thence near enough to Sackville Street to see if the rumours about its destruction were true, but here also we were halted by the military, and had to retrace our steps.

There was no news of any kind to be gathered from the people we talked to, nor had they even any rumours.

This was the first day I had been able to get even a short distance outside of my own quarter, and it seemed that the people of my quarter were more able in the manufacture of news or more imaginative than were the people who live in other parts of the city. We had no sooner struck into home parts than we found news. We were told that two of the Volunteer leaders had been shot. These were Pearse and Connolly. The latter was reported as lying in the Castle Hospital with a fractured thigh. Pearse was cited as dead with two hundred of his men, following their sally from the Post Office. The machine guns had caught them as they left, and none of them remained alive. The news seemed afterwards to be true except that instead of Pearse it was The O'Rahilly who had been killed. Pearse died later and with less excitement.

A man who had seen an English newspaper said that the Kut force had surrendered to the Turk, but that Verdun had not fallen to the Germans. The rumour was current also that a great naval battle had been fought whereat the German fleet had been totally destroyed with loss to the English of eighteen warships. It was said that among the captured Volunteers there had been a large body of Germans, but nobody believed it; and this rumour was inevitably followed by the tale that there were one hundred German submarines lying in the Stephen's Green pond.

At half-past two I met Mr. Commissioner Bailey, who told me that it was all over, and that the Volunteers were surrendering everywhere in the city. A motor car with two military officers, and two Volunteer leaders had driven to the College of Surgeons and been admitted. After a short interval

Madame Marckievicz marched out of the College at the head of about 100 men, and they had given up their arms; the motor car with the Volunteer leaders was driving to other strongholds, and it was expected that before nightfall the capitulations would be complete.

I started home, and on the way I met a man whom I had encountered some days previously, and from whom rumours had sprung as though he wove them from his entrails, as a spider weaves his web. He was no less provided on this occasion, and it was curious to listen to his tale of English defeats on every front. He announced the invasion of England in six different quarters, the total destruction of the English fleet, and the landing of immense German armies on the West coast of Ireland. He made these things up in his head. Then he repeated them to himself in a loud voice, and became somehow persuaded that they had been told to him by a well-informed stranger, and then he believed them and told them to everybody he met. Amongst other things Spain had declared war on our behalf, the Chilian Navy was hastening to our relief. For a pin he would have sent France flying westward all forgetful of her own war. A singular man truly, and as I do think the only thoroughly happy person in our city.

It is half-past three o'clock, and from my window the Republican flag can still be seen flying over Jacob's factory. There is occasional shooting, but the city as a whole is quiet. At a quarter to five o'clock a heavy gun boomed once. Ten minutes later there was heavy machine gun firing and much rifle shooting. In another ten minutes the flag at Jacob's was hauled down.

During the remainder of the night sniping and military replies were incessant, particularly in my street.

The raids have begun in private houses. Count Plunkett's house was entered by the military who remained there for a very long time. Passing home about two minutes after Proclamation hour I was pursued for the whole of Fitzwilliam Square by bullets. They buzzed into the roadway beside me, and the sound as they whistled near was curious. The sound is something like that made by a very swift saw, and one gets the impression that as well as being very swift they are very heavy.

Snipers are undoubtedly on the roofs opposite my house, and they are not asleep on these roofs. Possibly it is difficult to communicate with these isolated bands the news of their companions' surrender, but it is likely they will learn, by the diminution of fire in other quarters that their work is over.

In the morning on looking from my window I saw four policemen marching into the street. They were the first I had seen for a week. Soon now the military tale will finish, the police story will commence, the political story will recommence, and, perhaps, the weeks that follow this one will sow the seed of more hatred than so many centuries will be able to uproot again, for although Irish people do not greatly fear the military they fear the police, and they have very good reason to do so.

CHAPTER VIII.

THE INSURRECTION IS OVER.

THE Insurrection is over, and it is worth asking what has happened, how it has happened, and why it happened?

The first question is easily answered. The finest part of our city has been blown to smithereens, and burned into ashes. Soldiers amongst us who have served abroad say that the ruin of this quarter is more complete than any thing they have seen at Ypres, than anything they have seen anywhere in France or Flanders. A great number of our men and women and children, Volunteers and civilians confounded alike, are dead, and some fifty thousand men who have been moved with military equipment to our land are now being removed therefrom. The English nation has been disorganised no more than as they were affected by the transport of these men and material. That is what happened, and it is all that happened.

How it happened is another matter, and

one which, perhaps, will not be made clear for years. All we know in Dublin is that our city burst into a kind of spontaneous war; that we lived through it during one singular week, and that it faded away and disappeared almost as swiftly as it had come. The men who knew about it are, with two exceptions, dead, and these two exceptions are in gaol, and likely to remain there long enough. (Since writing one of these men has been shot.)

Why it happened is a question that may be answered more particularly. It happened because the leader of the Irish Party misrepresented his people in the English House of Parliament. On the day of the declaration of war between England and Germany he took the Irish case, weighty with eight centuries of history and tradition, and he threw it out of the window. He pledged Ireland to a particular course of action, and he had no authority to give this pledge and he had no guarantee that it would be met. The ramshackle intelligence of his party and his own emotional nature betrayed him and us and England. He swore Ireland to loyalty as if he had Ireland in his pocket, and could answer

for her. Ireland has never been disloyal to
England, not even at this epoch, because she
has never been loyal to England, and the pro-
fession of her National faith has been un-
wavering, has been known to every English
person alive, and has been clamant to all the
world beside.

Is it that he wanted to be cheered? He
could very easily have stated Ireland's case
truthfully, and have proclaimed a benevolent
neutrality (if he cared to use the grandilo-
quent words) on the part of this country. He
would have gotten his cheers, he would in a
few months have gotten Home Rule in return for Irish soldiers. He would have
received politically whatever England could
have safely given him. But, alas, these
carefulnesses did not chime with his emotional
moment. They were not magnificent enough
for one who felt that he was talking not to
Ireland or to England, but to the whole
gaping and eager earth, and so he pledged
his country's credit so deeply that he did not
leave her even one National rag to cover herself with.

After a lie truth bursts out, and it is no

longer the radiant and serene goddess we knew or hoped for—it is a disease, it is a moral syphilis and will ravage until the body in which it can dwell has been purged. Mr. Redmond told the lie and he is answerable to England for the violence she had to be guilty of, and to Ireland for the desolation to which we have had to submit. Without his lie there had been no Insurrection; without it there had been at this moment, and for a year past, an end to the " Irish question." Ireland must in ages gone have been guilty of abominable crimes or she could not at this juncture have been afflicted with a John Redmond.

He is the immediate cause of this our latest Insurrection—the word is big, much too big for the deed, and we should call it row, or riot, or squabble, in order to draw the fact down to its dimensions, but the ultimate blame for the trouble between the two countries does not fall against Ireland.

The fault lies with England, and in these days while an effort is being made (interrupted, it is true, by cannon) to found a better understanding between the two nations it is well that England should recognize what she has done to Ireland, and should try at least to atone for it. The situation can be explained almost in a phrase. We are a little country and you, a huge country, have persistently beaten us. We are a poor country and you, the richest country in the world, have persistently robbed us. That is the historical fact, and whatever national or political necessities are opposed in reply, it is true that you have never given Ireland any reason to love you, and you cannot claim her affection without hypocrisy or stupidity.

You think our people can only be tenacious in hate—it is a lie. Our historical memory is truly tenacious, but during the long and miserable tale of our relations you have never given us one generosity to remember you by, and you must not claim our affection or our devotion until you are worthy of them. We are a good people; almost we are the only Christian people left in the world, nor has any nation shown such forbearance towards their persecutor as we have always shown to you. No nation has forgiven its enemies as we have forgiven you, time after time down the miserable generations, the continuity of our forgiveness only equalled by the continuity of your ill-treatment. Between our two countries you have kept and protected a screen of traders and politicians who are just as truly your enemies as they are ours. In the end they will do most harm to you for we are by this vaccinated against misery but you are not, and the " loyalists " who sell their own country for a shilling will sell another country for a penny when the opportunity comes and safety with it.

Meanwhile do not always hasten your presents to us out of a gun. You have done it so often that your guns begin to bore us, and you have now an opportunity which may never occur again to make us your friends. There is no bitterness in Ireland against you on account of this war, and the lack of ill-feeling amongst us is entirely due to the more than admirable behaviour of the soldiers whom you sent over here. A peace that will last for ever can be made with Ireland if you wish to make it, but you must take her hand at once, for in a few months' time she will not open it to you; the old, bad relations will re-commence, the rancor will be born and grow, and another memory will be stored away in Ireland's capacious and retentive brain.

CHAPTER IX.

THE VOLUNTEERS.

THERE is much talk of the extraordinary organising powers displayed in the insurrection, but in truth there was nothing extraordinary in it. The real essence and singularity of the rising exists in its simplicity, and, saving for the courage which carried it out, the word extraordinary is misplaced in this context.

The tactics of the Volunteers as they began to emerge were reduced to the very skeleton of "strategy." It was only that they seized certain central and stragetical districts, garrisoned those and held them until they were put out of them. Once in their forts there was no further egress by the doors, and for purpose of entry and sortie they used the skylights and the roofs. On the roofs they had plenty of cover, and this cover conferred on them a mobility which was their chief asset, and which alone enabled them to protract the rebellion beyond the first day.

This was the entire of their home plan, and there is no doubt that they had studied Dublin roofs and means of inter-communication by roofs with the closest care. Further than that I do not think they had organised anything. But this was only the primary plan, and, unless they were entirely mad, there must have been a sequel to it which did not materialise, and which would have materialised but that the English Fleet blocked the way.

There is no doubt that they expected the country to rise with them, and they must have known what their own numbers were, and what chance they had of making a protracted resistance. The word " resistance " is the keyword of the rising, and the plan of holding out must have been rounded off with a date. At that date something else was to have happened which would relieve them.

There is not much else that could happen except the landing of German troops in Ireland or in England. It would have been, I think, immaterial to them where these were landed, but the reasoning seems to point to the fact that they expected and had arranged for such a landing, although on this point there is as yet no evidence.

The logic of this is so simple, so plausible, that it might be accepted without further examination, and yet further examination is necessary, for in a country like Ireland logic and plausibility are more often wrong than right. It may just as easily be that except for furnishing some arms and ammunition Germany was not in the rising at all, and this I prefer to believe. It had been current long before the rising that the Volunteers knew they could not seriously embarass England, and that their sole aim was to make such a row in Ireland that the Irish question would take the status of an international one, and on the discussion of terms of peace in the European war the claims of Ireland would have to be considered by the whole Council of Europe and the world.

That is, in my opinion, the metaphysic behind the rising. It is quite likely that they hoped for German aid, possibly some thousands of men, who would enable them to prolong the row, but I do not believe they expected German armies, nor do I think they would have welcomed these with any cordiality.

In this insurrection there are two things which are singular in the history of Irish risings. One is that there were no informers, or there were no informers among the chiefs. I did hear people say in the streets that two days before the rising they knew it was to come; they invariably added that they had not believed the news, and had laughed at it. A priest said the same thing in my hearing, and it may be that the rumour was widely spread, and that everybody, including the authorities, looked upon it as a joke.

The other singularity of the rising is the amazing silence in which it was fought. Nothing spoke but the guns; and the Volunteers on the one side and the soldiers on the other potted each other and died in whispers; it might have been said that both sides feared the Germans would hear them and take advantage of their preoccupation.

There is a third reason given for the rebellion, and it also is divorced from foreign plots. It is said, and the belief in Dublin was widespread, that the Government intended to raid the Volunteers and seize their arms. One remembers to-day the paper which Alderman Kelly read to the Dublin Corporation, and which purported to be State Instructions that the Military and Police should raid the Volunteers, and seize their arms and leaders. The Volunteers had sworn they would not permit their arms to be taken from them. A list of the places to be raided was given, and the news created something of a sensation in Ireland when it was published that evening. The Press, by instruction apparently, repudiated this document, but the Volunteers, with most of the public, believed it to be true, and it is more than likely that the rebellion took place in order to forestall the Government.

This is also an explanation of the rebellion, and is just as good a one as any other. It is the explanation which I believe to be the true one.

All the talk of German invasion and the landing of German troops in Ireland is so much nonsense in view of the fact that England is master of the seas, and that from a week before the war down to this date she has been the undisputed monarch of those ridges. During this war there will be no landing of troops in either England or Ireland unless Germany in the meantime can solve the problem of submarine transport. It is a problem which will be solved some day, for every problem can be solved, but it will hardly be during the progress of this war. The men at the head of the Volunteers were not geniuses, neither were they fools, and the difficulty of acquiring military aid from Germany must have seemed as insurmountable to them as it does to the Germans themselves. They rose because they felt that they had to do so, or be driven like sheep into the nearest police barracks, and be laughed at by the whole of Ireland as cowards and braggarts.

It would be interesting to know why, on the eve of the insurrection, Professor MacNeill resigned the presidency of the Volunteers. The story of treachery which was heard in the streets is not the true one, for men of his type are not traitors, and this statement may be dismissed without further comment or notice. One is left to imagine what can have happened during the conference which is said to have preceded the rising, and which ended with the resignation of Professor MacNeill.

This is my view, or my imagining, of what occurred. The conference was called because the various leaders felt that a hostile movement was projected by the Government, and that the times were exceedingly black for them. Neither Mr. Birrell nor Sir Mathew Nathan had any desire that there should be a conflict in Ireland during the war. This cannot be doubted. From such a conflict there might follow all kinds of political repercussions; but although the Government favoured the policy of *laissez faire*, there was a powerful military and political party in Ireland whose whole effort was towards the disarming and punishment of the Volunteers—particularly I should say the punishment of the Volunteers. I believe, or rather I imagine, that Professor MacNeill was approached at the instance of Mr. Birrell or Sir Mathew Nathan and assured that the Government did not meditate any move against his men, and that so long as his Volunteers remained quiet they would not be molested by the authorities. I would say that Professor MacNeill gave and accepted the necessary assurances, and that when he informed his conference of what had occurred, and found that they did not believe faith would be kept with them, he resigned in the dispairing hope that his action might turn them from a purpose which he considered lunatic, or, at least, by restraining a number of his followers from rising, he might limit the tale of men who would be uselessly killed.

He was not alone in his vote against a rising. The O'Rahilly and some others are reputed to have voted with him, but when insurrection was decided on, the O'Rahilly marched with his men, and surely a gallant man could not have done otherwise.

When the story of what occurred is authoritatively written (it may be written) I think that this will be found to be the truth of the matter, and that German intrigue and German money counted for so little in the insurrection as to be negligible.

CHAPTER X.

SOME OF THE LEADERS.

MEANWHILE the insurrection, like all its historical forerunners, has been quelled in blood. It sounds rhetorical to say so, but it was not quelled in peasoup or tisane. While it lasted the fighting was very determined, and it is easily, I think, the most considerable of Irish rebellions.

The country was not with it, for be it remembered that a whole army of Irishmen, possibly three hundred thousand of our race, are fighting with England instead of against her. In Dublin alone there is scarcely a poor home in which a father, a brother, or a son is not serving in one of the many fronts which England is defending. Had the country risen, and fought as stubbornly as the Volunteers did, no troops could have beaten them—well that is a wild statement, the heavy guns could always beat them—but from whatever angle Irish people consider this affair it must appear to them tragic and lamentable beyond expression, but not mean and not unheroic.

It was hard enough that our men in the English armies should be slain for causes which no amount of explanation will ever render less foreign to us, or even intelligible; but that our men who were left should be killed in Ireland fighting against the same England that their brothers are fighting for ties the question into such knots of contradiction as we may give up trying to unravel. We can only think—this has happened—and let it unhappen itself as best it may.

We say that the time always finds the man, and by it we mean : that when a responsibility is toward there will be found some shoulder to bend for the yoke which all others shrink from. It is not always nor often the great ones of the earth who undertake these burdens—it is usually the good folk, that gentle hierarchy who swear allegiance to mournfulness and the under dog, as others dedicate themselves to mutton chops and the easy nymph. It is not my intention to idealise any of the men who were concerned in this rebellion. Their country will, some few years hence, do that as adequately as she has done it for those who went before them.

Those of the leaders whom I knew were not great men, nor brilliant—that is they were more scholars than thinkers, and more thinkers than men of action; and I believe that in no capacity could they have attained to what is called eminence, nor do I consider they coveted any such public distinction as is noted in that word.

But in my definition they were good men—men, that is, who willed no evil, and whose movements of body or brain were unselfish and healthy. No person living is the worse off for having known Thomas MacDonagh, and I, at least, have never heard MacDonagh speak unkindly or even harshly of anything that lived. It has been said of him that his lyrics were epical; in a measure it is true, and it is true in the same measure that his death was epical. He was the first of the leaders who was tried and shot. It was not easy for him to die leaving behind two young children and a young wife, and the thought that his last moment must have been tormented by their memory is very painful. We are all fatalists when we strike against power, and I hope he put care from him as the soldiers marched him out.

The O'Rahilly also I knew, but not intimately, and I can only speak of a good humour, a courtesy, and an energy that never failed. He was a man of unceasing ideas and unceasing speech, and laughter accompanied every sound made by his lips.

Plunkett and Pearse I knew also, but not intimately. Young Plunkett, as he was always called, would never strike one as a militant person. He, like Pearse and MacDonagh, wrote verse, and it was no better nor worse than their's were. He had an appetite for quaint and difficult knowledge. He studied Egyptian and Sanscrit, and distant curious matter of that sort, and was interested in inventions and the theatre. He was tried and sentenced and shot.

As to Pearse, I do not know how to place him, nor what to say of him. If there was an idealist among the men concerned in this insurrection it was he, and if there was any person in the world less fitted to head an insurrection it was he also. I never could " touch" or sense in him the qualities which other men spoke of, and which made him military commandant of the rising. None of these men were magnetic in the sense that Mr. Larkin is magnetic, and I would have said that Pearse was less magnetic than any of the others. Yet it was to him and around him they clung.

Men must find some centre either of power or action or intellect about which they may group themselves, and I think that Pearse became the leader because his temperament was more profoundly emotional than any of the others. He was emotional not in a flighty, but in a serious way, and one felt more that he suffered than that he enjoyed.

He had a power; men who came into intimate contact with him began to act differently to their own desires and interests. His schoolmasters did not always receive their salaries with regularity. The reason that he did not pay them was the simple one that he had no money. Given by another man this explanation would be uneconomic, but from him it was so logical that even a child could

91

comprehend it. These masters did not always leave him. They remained, marvelling perhaps, and accepting, even with stupefaction, the theory that children must be taught, but that no such urgency is due towards the payment of wages. One of his boys said there was no fun in telling lies to Mr. Pearse, for, however outrageous the lie, he always believed it. He built and renovated and improved his school because the results were good for his scholars, and somehow he found builders to undertake these forlorn hopes.

It was not, I think, that he " put his trust in God," but that when something had to be done he did it, and entirely disregarded logic or economics or force. He said—such a thing has to be done and so far as one man can do it I will do it, and he bowed straightaway to the task.

It is mournful to think of men like these having to take charge of bloody and desolate work, and one can imagine them say, "Oh! cursed spite," as they accepted responsibility.

CHAPTER XI.

LABOUR AND THE INSURRECTION.

No person in Ireland seems to have exact information about the Volunteers, their aims, or their numbers. We know the names of the leaders now. They were recited to us with the tale of their execution; and with the declaration of a Republic we learned something of their aim, but the estimate of their number runs through the figures ten, thirty, and fifty thousand. The first figure is undoubtedly too slender, the last excessive, and something between fifteen and twenty thousand for all Ireland would be a reasonable guess.

Of these, the Citizen Army or Labour side of the Volunteers, would not number more than one thousand men, and it is with difficulty such a figure could be arrived at. Yet it is freely argued, and the theory will grow, that the causes of this latest insurrection should be sought among the labour problems of Dublin rather than in any national or patriotic sentiment, and this theory is buttressed by all the agile facts which such a theory would be furnished with.

It is an interesting view, but in my opinion it is an erroneous one.

That Dublin labour was in the Volunteer movement to the strength of, perhaps, two hundred men, may be true—it is possible there were more, but it is unlikely that a greater number, or, as many, of the Citizen Army marched when the order came. The overwhelming bulk of Volunteers were actuated by the patriotic ideal which is the heritage and the burden of almost every Irishman born out of the Unionist circle, and their connection with labour was much more manual than mental.

This view of the importance of labour to the Volunteers is held by two distinct and opposed classes.

Just as there are some who find the explanation of life in a sexual formula, so there is a class to whom the economic idea is very dear, and beneath every human activity they will discover the shock of wages and profit. It is truly there, but it pulls no more than its weight, and in Irish life the part played by labour has not yet been a weighty one, although on every view it is an important one. The labour idea in Ireland has not arrived. It is in process of " becoming," and when labour problems are mentioned in this country a party does not come to the mind, but two men only—they are Mr. Larkin and James Connolly, and they are each in their way exceptional and curious men.

There is another class who implicate labour, and they do so because it enables them to urge that as well as being grasping and nihilistic, Irish labour is disloyal and treacherous.

The truth is that labour in Ireland has not yet succeeded in organising anything—not even discontent. It is not self-conscious to any extent, and, outside of Dublin, it scarcely appears to exist. The national imagination is not free to deal with any other subject than that of freedom, and part of the policy of our " masters " is to see that we be kept busy with politics instead of social ideas. From their standpoint the policy is admirable, and up to the present it has thoroughly succeeded.

THE INSURRECTION IN DUBLIN

One does not hear from the lips of the Irish workingman, even in Dublin, any of the affirmations and rejections which have long since become the commonplaces of his comrades in other lands. But on the subject of Irish freedom his views are instantly forthcoming, and his desires are explicit, and, to a degree, informed. This latter subject they understand and have fabricated an entire language to express it, but the other they do not understand nor cherish, and they are not prepared to die for it.

It is possibly true that before any movement can attain to really national proportions there must be, as well as the intellectual ideal which gives it utterance and a frame, a sense of economic misfortune to give it weight, and when these fuse the combination may well be irresistible. The organised labour discontent in Ireland, in Dublin, was not considerable enough to impose its aims or its colours on the Volunteers, and it is the labour ideal which merges and disappears in the national one. The reputation of all the leaders of the insurrection, not excepting Connolly, is that they were intensely patriotic

Irishmen, and also, but this time with the exception of Connolly, that they were not particularly interested in the problems of labour.

The great strike of two years ago remained undoubtedly as a bitter and lasting memory with Dublin labour—perhaps, even, it was not so much a memory as a hatred. Still, it was not hatred of England which was evoked at that time, nor can the stress of their conflict be traced to an English source. It was hatred of local traders, and, particularly, hatred of the local police, and the local powers and tribunals, which were arrayed against them.

One can without trouble discover reasons why they should go on strike again, but by no reasoning can I understand why they should go into rebellion against England, unless it was that they were patriots first and trade unionists a very long way afterwards.

I do not believe that this combination of the ideal and the practical was consummated in the Dublin insurrection, but I do believe that the first step towards the formation of such a party has now been taken, and that if, years hence, there should be further trouble in Ireland such trouble will not be so easily dealt with as this one has been.

It may be that further trouble will not arise, for the co-operative movement, which is growing slowly but steadily in Ireland, may arrange our economic question, and, incidentally, our national question also—that is if the English people do not decide that the latter ought to be settled at once.

James Connolly had his heart in both the national and the economic camp, but he was a great-hearted man, and could afford to extend his affections where others could only dissipate them.

There can be no doubt that his powers of orderly thinking were of great service to the Volunteers, for while Mr. Larkin was the magnetic centre of the Irish labour movement, Connolly was its brains. He has been sentenced to death for his part in the insurrection, and for two days now he has been dead.

He had been severely wounded in the fighting, and was tended, one does not doubt with great care, until he regained enough strength to stand up and be shot down again.

Others are dead also. I was not acquainted with them, and with Connolly I was not more than acquainted. I had met him twice many months ago, but other people were present each time, and he scarcely uttered a word on either of these occasions. I was told that he was by nature silent. He was a man who can be ill-spared in Ireland, but labour, throughout the world, may mourn for him also.

A doctor who attended on him during his last hours says that Connolly received the sentence of his death quietly. He was to be shot on the morning following the sentence. This gentleman said to him :

" Connolly, when you stand up to be shot, will you say a prayer for me ? "

Connolly replied :

" I will."

His visitor continued :

" Will you say a prayer for the men who are shooting you ? "

" I will," said Connolly, " and I will say a prayer for every good man in the world who is doing his duty."

He was a steadfast man in all that he undertook. We may be sure he steadfastly kept that promise. He would pray for others, who had not time to pray for himself, as he had worked for others during the years when he might have worked for himself.

CHAPTER XII.

THE IRISH QUESTIONS.

THERE is truly an Irish question. There are two Irish questions, and the most important of them is not that which appears in our newspapers and in our political propaganda.

The first is international, and can be stated shortly. It is the desire of Ireland to assume control of her national life. With this desire the English people have professed to be in accord, and it is at any rate so thoroughly understood that nothing further need be made of it in these pages.

The other Irish question is different, and less simply described. The difficulty about it is that it cannot be approached until the question of Ireland's freedom has by some means been settled, for this ideal of freedom has captured the imagination of the race. It rides Ireland like a nightmare, thwarting or preventing all civilising or cultural work in this country, and it is not too much to say that Ireland cannot even begin to live until that obsession and fever has come to an end, and her imagination has been set free to do the work which imagination alone can do— Imagination is intelligent kindness—we have sore need of it.

The second question might plausibly be called a religious one. It has been so called, and, for it is less troublesome to accept an idea than to question it, the statement has been accepted as truth—but it is untrue, and it is deeply and villianously untrue. No lie in Irish life has been so persistent and so mischievous as this one, and no political lie has ever been so ingeniously, and malevolently exploited.

There is no religious intolerance in Ireland except that which is political. I am not a member of the Catholic Church, and am not inclined to be the advocate of a religious system which my mentality dislikes, but I have never found real intolerance among my fellow-countrymen of that religion. I have found it among Protestants. I will limit that statement, too. I have found it among some Protestants. But outside of the North of Ireland there is no religious question, and in the North it is fundamentally more political than religious.

All thinking is a fining down of one's ideas, and thus far we have come to the statement of Ireland's second question. It is not Catholic or Nationalist, nor have I said that it is entirely Protestant and Unionist, but it is on the extreme wing of this latter party that responsibility must be laid. It is difficult, even for an Irishman living in Ireland, to come on the real political fact which underlies Irish Protestant politics, and which fact has consistently opposed and baffled every attempt made by either England or Ireland to come to terms. There is such a fact, and clustered around it is a body of men whose hatred of their country is persistent and deadly and unexplained.

One may make broad generalisations on the apparent situation and endeavour to solve it by those. We may say that loyalty to England is the true centre of their action. I will believe it, but only to a point. Loyalty to England does not inevitably include this active hatred, this blindness, this withering of all sympathy for the people among whom one is born, and among whom one has lived in peace, for they have lived in peace amongst us. We may say that it is due to the idea of privilege and the desire for power. Again, I will accept it up to a point—but these are cultural obsessions, and they cease to act when the breaking-point is reached.

I know of only two mental states which are utterly without bowels or conscience. These are cowardice and greed. Is it to a synthesis of these states that this more than mortal enmity may be traced? What do they fear, and what is it they covet? What can they redoubt in a country which is practically crimeless, or covet in a land that is almost as bare as a mutton bone? They have mesmerised themselves, these men, and have imagined into our quiet air brigands and thugs and titans, with all the other notabilities of a tale for children.

I do not think that this either will tell the tale, but I do think there is a story to be told —I imagine an esoteric wing to the Unionist Party. I imagine that Party includes a secret organisation—they may be Orangemen, they

may be Masons, and, if there be such, I would
dearly like to know what the metaphysic of
their position is, and how they square it with
any idea of humanity or social life. Meantime, all this is surmise, and I, as a novelist,
have a notoriously flighty imagination, and
am content to leave it at that.

But this secondary Irish question is not so
terrible as it appears. It is terrible now, it
would not be terrible if Ireland had national
independence.

The great protection against a lie is—not
to believe it; and Ireland, in this instance,
has that protection. The claims made by the
Unionist Wing do not rely solely on the religious base. They use all the arguments. It is,
according to them, unsafe to live in Ireland.
(Let us leave this insurrection of a week out
of the question.) Life is not safe in Ireland.
Property shivers in terror of daily or nightly
appropriation. Other, undefined, but even
more woeful glooms and creeps, wriggle
stealthily abroad.

These things are not regarded in Ireland,
and, in truth, they are not meat for Irish con-
sumption. Irish judges are presented with

white gloves with a regularity which may even be annoying to them, and were it not for political trouble they would be unable to look their salaries in the face. The Irish Bar almost weep in chorus at the words "Land Act," and stare, not dumbly, on destitution. These tales are meant for England and are sent there. They will cease to be exported when there is no market for them, and these men will perhaps end by becoming patriotic and social when they learn that they do not really command the Big Battalions. But Ireland has no protection against them while England can be thrilled by their nonsense, and while she is willing to pound Ireland to a jelly on their appeal. Her only assistance against them is freedom.

There are certain simplicities upon which all life is based. A man finds that he is hungry and the knowledge enables him to go to work for the rest of his life. A man makes the discovery (it has been a discovery to many) that he is an Irishman, and the knowledge simplifies all his subsequent political action. There is this comfort about being an Irishman, you can be entirely Irish, and claim thus to be as complete as a pebble or a star. But no Irish person can hope to be more than a muletto Englishman, and if that be an ambition and an end it is not an heroic one.

But there is an Ulster difficulty, and no amount of burking it will solve it. It is too generally conceived among Nationalists that the attitude of Ulster towards Ireland is rooted in ignorance and bigotry. Allow that both of these bad parts are included in the Northern outlook, they do not explain the Ulster standpoint; and nothing can explain the attitude of official Ireland *vis-a-vis* with Ulster.

What has the Irish Party ever done to allay Northern prejudice, or bring the discontented section into line with the rest of Ireland? The answer is pathetically complete. They have done nothing. Or, if they have done anything, it was only that which would set every Northerner grinding his teeth in anger. At a time when Orangeism was dying they raised and marshalled the Hibernians, and we have the Ulsterman's answer to the Hibernians in the situation by which we are confronted to-day. If the Party had even a little statesmanship among them they would for the past ten years have marched up and down the North explaining and mollifying and courting the Black Northerner. But, like good Irishmen, they could not tear themselves away from England, and they paraded that country where parade was not so urgent, and they made orations there until the mere accent of an Irishman must make Englishmen wail for very boredom.

Some of that parade might have gladdened the eyes of the Belfast citizens; a few of those orations might have assisted the men of Derry to comprehend that, for the good of our common land, Home Rule and the unity of a nation was necessary if only to rid the country of these blatherers.

Let the Party explain why, among their political duties, they neglected the duty of placating Ulster in their proper persons. Why, in short, they boycotted Ulster and permitted political and religious and racial antagonism to grow inside of Ireland unchecked by any word from them upon that ground. Were they afraid "nuts" would be thrown at them? Whatever they dreaded, they gave Ulster the widest of wide berths, and wherever else they were visible and audible, they were silent and unseen in that part of Ireland.

The Ulster grievance is ostensibly religious; but safeguards on this count are so easily created and applied that this issue might almost be left out of account. The real difficulty is economic, and it is a tangled one. But unless profit and loss are immediately discernible the soul of man is not easily stirred by an accountant's tale, and therefore the religious banner has been waved for our kinsfolk of Ulster, and under the sacred emblem they are fighting for what some people call mammon, but which may be in truth just plain bread and butter.

Before we can talk of Ireland a nation we must make her one. A nation, politically speaking, is an aggregation of people whose interests are identical; and the interests of Ulster with the rest of Ireland rather than being identical are antagonistic. It is England orders and pays for the Belfast ships, and it is to Britain or under the goodwill of the British power that Ulster conducts her huge woollen trade. Economically the rest of Ireland scarcely exists for Ulster, and whoever insists on regarding the Northern question from an ideal plane is wasting his own time and the time of everyone who listens to him. The safeguards which Ulster will demand, should events absolutely force her to it, may sound political or religious, they will be found essentially economic, and the root of them all will be a watertight friendship with England, and anything that smells, however distantly, of hatred for England will be a true menace to Ulster. We must swallow England if Ulster is to swallow us, and until that fact becomes apparent to Ireland the Ulster problem cannot be even confronted, let alone solved.

The words Sinn Fein mean " Ourselves," and it is of ourselves I write in this chapter. More urgent than any political emancipation is the drawing together of men of good will in the endeavour to assist their necessitous land. Our eyes must be withdrawn from the ends of the earth and fixed on that which is around us and which we can touch. No politician will talk to us of Ireland if by any trick he can avoid the subject. His tale is still of Westminster and Chimborazo and the Mountains of the Moon. Irishmen must begin to think for themselves and of themselves, instead of expending energy on causes too distant to be assisted or hindered by them. I believe that our human material is as good as will be found in the world. No better, perhaps, but not worse. And I believe that all but local politics are unfruitful and soul-destroying. We have an island that is called little. It is more than twenty times too spacious for our needs, and we will not have explored the last of it in our children's lifetime. We have more problems to resolve in our towns and cities than many generations of minds will get tired of striving with. Here is the world, and all that perplexes or delights the world is here also. Nothing is lost. Not even brave men. They have been used. From this day the great adventure opens for Ireland. The Volunteers are dead, and the call is now for volunteers.

AFTERWORD

JOHN A. MURPHY

'FROM this day', concludes Stephens, 'the great adventure opens for Ireland. The Volunteers are dead, and the call now is for volunteers'. The executions and mass arrests were followed by a great swing of support in nationalist Ireland to the side of the survivors and for the cause they represented. The emergence of a new national leader, Eamon de Valera, was due in no small measure to the aura of glamour that surrounded him as a surviving hero of Easter Week. Throughout 1917, the Volunteers and Sinn Féin were re-organized, and ostensibly harmonious relations were established between the two bodies, though the tensions between the military men and the politicians simmered beneath the surface in the period of nationalist resurgence that followed. What really decided popular support for Sinn Féin was that organization's skilful direction, indeed exploitation, of the widespread opposition to the threat of conscription in 1918. The December, 1918, general election resulted in the rout of the old parliamentary party and in a landslide victory for Sinn Féin which thereupon set up an Irish parliament, Dáil Eireann. The Dáil claimed jurisdiction over all of Ireland but was completely rejected by the Unionist north-east.

Though Sinn Féin had neither the intention nor the mandate to assert Irish independence by force of arms, its hopes of securing international recognition at the Peace Conference proved unfounded and, from 1919, the Volunteers moved insensibly into armed combat with the Royal Irish Constabulary, its auxiliary units and the regular armed forces of the Crown. Though the Volunteers were under the nominal control of Dáil Eireann and its 'Republican' government, the initiative in the War of Independence lay almost entirely with the Volunteers, or the Irish Republican Army, as they came to be called. As the Anglo-Irish conflict intensified during 1920 and the early part of 1921, terror was met with terror and only a few short years after the nineteenthcentury theatrical setpiece of the Easter Rising, Ireland experienced the ruthlessness of twentieth century guerrilla warfare and anti-guerrilla repression.

Military stalemate, growing repugnance at the atrocities perpetrated in the name of the Crown, and the increasing clamour of British, Commonwealth, American and world liberal opinion—all combined to bring about a truce in the summer of 1921 and the beginning of negotiations which led to the Anglo-Irish Treaty at the end of that year. By then, the place of Unionist Ulster in the United Kingdom was secure behind the borders of a new six-county Northern Ireland statelet, though Sinn Féin fondly believed that partition was only a temporary arrangement. The Treaty set up an Irish Free State, with a self-governing dominion status, for the remaining twenty-six counties. Though this State was to evolve within a short period to complete sovereignty, as its supporters predicted, the Treaty settlement was opposed in tragic civil war (1922-23) by those who claimed that the compromise was a cynical betrayal of the Republic proclaimed in 1916 and of the men who had fought and died for it in Easter Week and in the War of Independence.

AFTERWORD

Thus, as the modern Irish state was painfully born, the presence of the 1916 ghosts ('MacDonagh's bony thumb' in Yeats's evocative phrase) was everywhere palpable, then and for many a year to come.